A Parent's Guide to 4th Grade

How to Ensure Your Child's Success

Ricki Winegardner

LEARNINGEXPRESS

NEW YORK

Copyright © 2001 LearningExpress, LLC.

Library of Congress Cataloging-in-Publication Data:
Winegardner, Ricki.
 A parent's guide to 4th grade/ by Ricki Winegardner—1st ed..
  p. com.
 ISBN 1-57685-375-6
 1. Fourth Grade (Education)—United States. 2. Education, Elementary—Parent
participation—United States. I. Title: Parent's Guide to fourth grade. II. Title.
 LB1571 .W56 2001
 372.24'2—dc21

                 00-067425

All rights reserved under International and Pan-American Copyright Conventions.
Published in the United States by Learning Express, LLC, New York.

Reprinted materials:
Copyright © 2001 The President's Challenge; see pages 39–40.

Printed in the United States of America
9 8 7 6 5 4 3 2 1
First Edition

For more information or to place an order, contact LearningExpress at:
900 Broadway
Suite 604
New York, NY 10003

Or visit us at:
 www.learnatest.com

Contents

Acknowledgments

HAVE you ever sat quietly, late at night, when the house is quiet, and counted blessings? I have.

Blessings sometimes come in the way of people—people who you spend hours with each day, and people whom you have never gotten the opportunity to share coffee and bagels with.

I have shared pizza with a blessing named Ross, laughs with a blessing named Seth, and nail polish with a blessing named Sara. I share my life with a blessing named Darin.

Someday I will share hugs with a blessing named Sherry, high fives with a blessing named Faith, and will "beam" with a blessing named Janice.

There are two blessings who can also be considered your blessings as well, since their editorial expertise was instrumental to the successful completion of this book. Jennifer and Sandy—how would I ever do this without you?

Tonight the house is quiet, and I am surrounded by my blessings.

1

Welcome to 4th Grade
Here Come the Big Kids!

IT'S OFFICIAL! The summer break is quickly waning, and although the third grade year was finished just a short time ago, an exciting new school year is just around the corner. Now that your child is heading to fourth grade, he is a bona fide big kid.

Fourth grade is often referred to as a transitional grade among educators, however this characterization of fourth grade lends itself well to a child's social, physical, and emotional growth as well. Because the status of big kid also means exposure to a new world that is often uncomfortable, and can become dangerous, the issues faced by the parent of a fourth grader are unique in their complexity and maturity. Puberty is just around the corner, and this brings with it a host of issues that can fill even the most seasoned and well-informed parent with a major case of nerves. Gone are the days of simplicity; welcome to the world of fourth grade.

Children who may have skated easily through previous grades may discover that fourth grade academics offer new challenges, and perhaps a few hurdles. While the third grader started making her way down the path toward serious studies, the fourth grade student will be expected to start the year running, prepared to work from the very first day back to school. You might notice that this year's classrooms are filled with a vast array of maps, charts, and diagrams, all essential to the more advanced studies covered in grade four. For the first time in her school career, your child may be changing classrooms for each of her major subjects. Throughout the day, she may visit several classrooms and be exposed to very different teaching styles.

With all of these changes, a sense of concern and uncertainty may overwhelm you as you think of the many twists and turns that your fourth grader's academic and social path may take this year. Uncertainty breeds fear, and that may explain the apprehension you are feeling as you think about the increased homework load, the more detailed subject matters being covered, and your child's growing awareness of complex social issues. These feelings are very natural and expected in parents of fourth graders. If you are one of the many uneasy parents of a fourth grade child, take heart—you have a lot of company. Fortunately today's world offers a wide variety of resources to parents who find themselves spending a significant amount of time wondering what they can do to ensure their child's educational success. This book is one such resource.

YOUR CHILD, THE STUDENT

THERE are many different learning environments, and none of them are inherently right or wrong. The most important factor to consider in any learning environment is that the student receives the educational and emotional support necessary to ensure educational success. While some children attend public schools in large urban areas, others are attending small rural schools. Some children attend private schools with religious affiliations, while others attend private schools without regard to specific faith or belief. Homeschooling is also increasing in popularity throughout all socioeconomic groups. By the time your child has entered fourth grade, you have probably settled on a particular educational environment. Although each of the environments mentioned have unique teaching methods, the basic goals of fourth grade are common across all of them.

If your child is attending an elementary school that includes kindergarten through fourth grade, your child is beginning his last year of elementary school. Other elementary schools continue through sixth grade, which equates to several more grades until your child joins the ranks of the middle- or junior-high school students. While your fourth grader may or may not be the oldest child in his school, most of the other students in elementary school are younger than he is. You may believe that your fun-loving fourth grade child does not notice trivialities such as this, but don't be so sure. Take note of the confidence in his step, the way he prides himself in leading younger children to the school bus or across the crosswalk. He walks a little taller nowadays, and contrary to the speed at which he is growing out of his clothes, this new and more mature child is not completely attributable to the growth spurt he may be experiencing. This grown-up feeling that your child will enjoy as a fourth grader could fill you with mixed emotions. This mixture of emotions churn inside you as you beam with pride one moment and explode with frustration only minutes later as he gains confidence and maturity while awkwardly attempting to spread his wings.

Although terms like "transitional grade," "standardized tests," and "educational success" may cause parents to feel like they are outsiders observing their child's educational experience from afar, it is important that parents remember that they are their child's first and best teacher. Growing children naturally look to their parents or primary caregivers for guidance in new or difficult situations; your fourth grader has been doing this since birth. We have all enjoyed our toddlers and pre-school children when they have mimicked us. A chubby-faced three year old sitting intently in front of a coloring book pretending to write like a grown up while her parent is writing out the monthly bills is one such example. Another example of this sort of mimicking or play-learning is the pre-school child who attempts to help a parent set the table for the evening meal. As our children have grown, they have learned more complex, and sometimes more subtle lessons from parents. If you listen closely to your child as he speaks, you may hear a familiar cadence to his voice, or perhaps a familiar and often-used phrase. Now listen to yourself. Do you hear the same cadence in your voice? Is there a particular set of words that you use often? You see, you have been teaching your child all along! It is important for you to realize what an important influence you are in your child's educational experience, and how that influence can have a direct relationship to your fourth grader's educational success.

While "transitional grade" and "standardized tests" are covered in depth later in the book, the term "educational success" is integrated throughout.

Because of the use of this term in almost every chapter, it is imperative that you have a solid idea of what the term "educational success" means. Educational success does not necessarily mandate that your son or daughter must maintain an "A" average in all subjects. Educational success is not meant to imply that your child's name will be found regularly on the honor roll. Educational success does not mean that your child will be destined to win all the popularity contests. What educational success *does* mean is that you, your child, and the teacher(s) assigned to your child will work together to provide the best overall experience for your child, keeping his delightfully special gifts and needs in mind, working toward goals, and maintaining a positive attitude toward education.

Your fourth grader's confidence may translate to a greater sense of freedom for you. She may not want or need your help with standard homework assignments. Although you may be fully aware that she may be capable of completing assignments without your constant intervention, you will still want to make yourself readily available to her—should she begin to struggle. Your fourth grader may cringe if you try to help her with tasks before she asks for your assistance, especially in the presence of her peers. She is determined to believe that your unsolicited help reduces her to the ranks of the "little kids."

One of the rewards of parenting is that you have the opportunity to observe the metamorphosis of your child. Caterpillar, to chrysalis, to butterfly—you have front row seats to a fabulous process of nature. This year you will be treated to a view through a tiny window to the adult she will become eventually. Is she a natural born leader? Is she extremely self-motivated? Does she choose a group and then become a willing and active contributor to the group? Perhaps she is more comfortable to test the waters before immersing herself in new situations, or she may toss herself into the pool of activities with unabashed exuberance.

Educational Cornerstones

Ensuring the educational success of your child means that you must first be aware of the subject matter being covered during this difficult year. Fourth grade is serious business. While your child will spend a small amount of time reviewing lessons learned in third grade, he should be ready to dive into new subject matter within a short time of returning to school. As you may have noticed, each grade in elementary school builds upon the previous. Remember that in third grade your child started reading to learn instead of learning to read. The fourth grade student will exercise this skill in depth, and may find himself struggling in many classes, including mathematics, if he is not proficient at basic reading skills. Your fourth grader should however, possess the basic skills of reading comprehension. Science, History, and Social Studies take on a new focus this year. Fourth grade students suddenly become exposed to new topics that will spark their interest and inspire their imaginations.

Some Highlights of Learning

While many basic skills already have been mastered before your child enters fourth grade, there is still a lot of learning to do. The fourth grade child will add to her toolbox of skills and learn to use several skills in conjunction to create and complete more advanced projects. Although the list below highlights of some of the more advanced skills your fourth grader will master this year, it is important that you remember that this list is only a general guideline. Your child may have already mastered some of these skills, or may be a little behind in building her skill set. Remember that because this is merely a list of guidelines, all ranges of the spectrum are to be expected, and by the end of the year, your child should be adept at the majority of the tasks listed. Measure your child's progress by checking off each skill as he masters it.

SKILLS CHECKLIST

- ❐ Have a complete understanding of large numbers (larger than 1,000)
- ❐ Attain a comfort level with addition, subtraction, multiplication, and division of whole numbers
- ❐ Have a basic understanding of simple fractions and decimals
- ❐ Be able to identify and understand relationships between a variety of geometric figures
- ❐ Establish advanced writing skills, from creating a rough draft, through editing, and producing a final product
- ❐ Use research tools such as encyclopedias, atlases, newspapers, and dictionaries
- ❐ The ability to intelligently surmise the meaning of an unfamiliar word using context clues
- ❐ Independently locate information to assist with research projects

Signs of Academic Difficulty

Although it is natural to expect that your child will excel in all subjects, it is not uncommon for fourth grade to be difficult for students, even those who have seemingly breezed through grades one through three. Some signs of academic difficulty include the inability to:

- ➤ Organize time efficiently
- ➤ Behave appropriately
- ➤ Master a solid reading vocabulary
- ➤ Handle basic math facts
- ➤ Study for tests

If you are unsure of your child's progress in fourth grade, or are noticing that she is having trouble mastering some of the basic skills, you might want to arrange a meeting with all or some of the members of your child's educational team. This meeting will provide you the opportunity to describe some of the difficulties your child is exhibiting at home. Keep an open mind during this meeting, remembering that the other members of your child's educational team may or may not be aware of the difficulties you are concerned about.

. . . Fourth graders are stuck between being babies and being teenagers. It really starts in third grade, but becomes more obvious in fourth. They have to work harder and take their school work more seriously.

—A TEACHER ASSISTANT IN NORTH CAROLINA

Social Skills

Your child has already experienced many phases of social growth. You may remember when you were the center of his universe. Slowly your child's world changed and he began to notice that there were others in the world that were very important to him, as well. As difficult as it may be to admit, you may also remember slight pangs of jealousy as your child seemed to dote on a special teacher. This year's child is moving into yet another phase of social development.

The fourth grade child enjoys being part of a group. The whole is more important than each of the parts to a fourth grade child. This is to say that he is interested in doing things for himself, but prefers those things that he can do with his entire peer group. He revels in team play, group activities, and class projects. He is gaining a better sense of self, and is becoming more aware of how he fits into the group. Although he indeed enjoys friendships and group activities, he is more apt to make value decisions based on lessons learned in the past. He will begin to make decisions based on how he feels, as opposed to how that decision will affect other people. Values that you instilled in your child over the past years are becoming more apparent. For example, the fourth grader may consciously make the decision to not engage in rough-housing on the playground with a group of friends simply because he knows it is not the right thing to do. As the fourth grader finds himself more exposed to difficult situations, and faced with making difficult life decisions, he will draw on his sense of right and wrong.

Even More Transitions

Your fourth grader may be beginning some very important physiological changes. Some children begin the awkward path toward adulthood in fourth grade. As difficult as it may be to imagine, puberty may touch your child this year. As you well know, the onset of puberty can further complicate any difficulties your child may already be having. If your child is socially struggling, she may become withdrawn as she starts to blossom into a more womanly figure. If your child is very active, he may become the object of teasing if body odor suddenly becomes apparent. The onset of puberty also brings with it moodiness. If your fourth grader suddenly experiences meltdowns for no apparent reason, you may want to consider the hormonal changes that could be occurring. For these reasons, it is important that you are prepared to engage your child in honest discussion about puberty, body changes, and good personal hygiene.

YOU, THE PARENT

ALTHOUGH it is natural for a parent to feel as though their role in their child's life is lessening with each candle on the birthday cake, the truth is that your child needs you this year. Your fourth grader needs you to notice when he is frustrated with his homework. He needs you to discuss the world of violence he sees around him. He needs you to show him productive and constructive activities to keep his mind and body busy.

Do not underestimate your influence on your child. While your fourth grader may appear to be more interested in socializing with friends, remember that she still needs you and relishes the moments that you spend together. In the past it may have seemed easier to be involved with your child. You were one of your child's favorite playmates, her best friend, and her parent. This year your role will be different. While you are still one of your child's favorite people, she may be less willing to show her affections. She will stubbornly show her independence, and then come back to you when she realizes that she may have bitten off more than she could chew. Allowing her to struggle to find her own way, come to her own solutions, and make her own mistakes is part of the growth experience. She will come to you willingly when she needs your help.

Where Do I Fit In?

Parents of fourth grade children are less likely than their third grade counterparts to be active in their child's school life. As children get older, parents sometimes believe that they are no longer necessary participants at school and social activities. This misconception could not be further from the truth. Across the board, teachers of older children echo their wishes that more parents would be actively involved in their child's education. There are several different ways that parents can be actively involved in their child's academic and social growth. These parental involvement styles fall into one of the following four categories.

Political
The politically involved parent often runs for a seat on the local school board. This parent will assist in making decisions that affect the student body and

community as a whole. Budgetary needs are outlined, school policies are created and ratified, and personnel issues dealt with by the politically involved parent. If not seated on the school board, this parent may find other political avenues to affect the local public school system. This could include running for community government seats, or lobbying those who are in power. This parent writes letters to the editor, attends school board meetings, and is often the author of petitions.

Organizational

Similar to the politically involved parent, the organizationally involved parent is part of an established group of decision makers. These parents are members or officers in the Parent-Teacher Association, Parent-Teacher Organization, Parent-Teacher-Student Organization, or Parents Club at their child's school. Meant to be a voice for parents, these organizations promote open communication between the entire educational team. These organizations often sponsor fund-raising events to provide activities, technology, or educational supplies to the school. These groups of organizationally involved parents fund many student field trips.

Volunteers/Aides

The volunteer parent spends time at school, school events, or other volunteer positions. This parent can also be found coaching children's sports, teaching Sunday school, or leading a den of Boy Scouts or troop of Girl Scouts. This parent will be seen sitting at the back of the classroom organizing worksheets for tomorrow's lessons, or in the library shelving books. With school budgets being decimated, and community programs being downgraded, the volunteer is becoming more important than ever. You will see the volunteering parent chaperoning fundraising events, manning the bake sale, or providing refreshments at a civic event. The volunteer parental involvement style is often entered into by accident. Your inquisitiveness about your child's school life leads you to attend special functions, and "since you are going anyway . . ." becomes a wonderful excuse to lend a helping hand. You coach softball because your daughter is playing on the team, or become a den parent for your son's Boy Scout den. Remember that being a volunteer is not only helpful to your school or civic organization, but you are also providing your children with a wonderful example of community service.

Private

Although this is the only parental involvement style that does not put the parent in the public eye, it is extremely important. The privately involved parent spends time listening to their child, assisting with homework, and educating themselves to better help their child succeed. Not a day goes by where this parent does not have at least one thought of teaching their child through a life lesson. This parent lives within each of us; we only need to know how to tap into that person to become the best privately involved parent possible. Your interest in this book automatically qualifies you for this parental involvement style.

No parent fits all of the parental involvement styles listed above, but the majority of parents fit no less than one of the styles. Reading this book shows that you are indeed interested in your child's education and are searching for ways to become involved in order to ensure his educational success. Choose the methods of involvement that you feel most comfortable with, and give your child the chance to succeed.

Why Should I Be Involved?

Take a minute to look out your window or across the room at your child. It is amazing how the bundle of joy you brought home nine or ten years ago has grown into a wide-eyed and curious fourth grader, isn't it? When our children are handed to us—gifts sent to us for nurturing and teaching—we treasure every minute spent with them. Now that your child is a fourth grader, he is halfway to becoming an adult. Although you will always be instrumental to the lives of your children, you are now entrenched in the years where your children are most directly influenced by you, your behavior and actions. Decisions that you make now will remain as indelible etchings on your child's memory.

Children of this age appreciate the extra effort it takes for a parent to be involved in their education. Mind you, they will not always show their appreciation, but fourth grade children understand community service and will appreciate your involvement as not only good parenting, but also good community service. As unsettling as it is to think about, your fourth grader may be exposed to some of the unpleasant realities of today's society. Drugs, alcohol, and violence are no longer unknowns to your child. It may shock you to know that your fourth grader may already know children who smoke or abuse controlled substances. This is a disturbing fact of living in today's society.

The good news is that studies have shown that being involved in your child's life, both socially and academically, positively affects your child's chances of growing into a healthy adult relatively unscathed by these unpleasant forces in today's living.

Self-Doubt and Negativity

The National PTA reminds parents that "Research shows that when parents are involved in students' education, those students generally have higher grades and test scores, better attendance, and more consistently completed homework." This is not to say that your child will always be a willing partner in your involvement, but you should make every effort to find ways to include yourself in your child's academic and social journey. This could prove difficult if your educational experience was less than ideal. You may find yourself struggling to feel comfortable as part of your child's educational team. Whenever you feel incompetent, inadequate, or unable to be a productive member of the team, ask your child's teachers how they feel about parental involvement. Most educators will expel an exasperated, "I wish MORE parents were involved!"

YOUR TEAMMATE, THE TEACHER

Your Partner in Education

MANY fourth grade children will visit a multiplicity of teachers throughout the day. It is not unusual for a fourth grader to have a homeroom teacher, a different teacher for each of the major subjects (Math, Reading, Science, Social Studies), and then several other teachers who specialize in subjects such as Art and Music. As you can see, your child's educational team is growing.

Teachers of fourth grade children will expect that your child will come to school ready to work. The fourth grade teacher will expect your child to be responsible and capable of dealing with day-to-day tasks with ease. Now that your child has graduated from the primary grades, you will find that the teachers are less likely to coddle their students. There is good reason for this. The fourth grade teacher is often very task oriented, and will be teaching your child life lessons such as time management, as well as organizational and peer interaction skills.

Try not to label teachers as "mean" or unfair to your fourth grader. The fourth grade child is extremely aware of his parents' ideas and opinions. While your fourth grader may not always agree with your assessment of his teachers, he will definitely be influenced by your attitudes. Being a bit less timid this year, he may actually feel compelled to share with his teacher what his parents think. Today's educator finds that he is not only responsible for teaching the basics of academics, but also fulfills the role of surrogate parent, policeman, social worker, counselor, and healthcare provider. A national study of teachers of children in grades one through four showed that teachers are spending an average of 11.6 hours a week on activities outside of teaching. These activities included, but were not limited to tutoring, staff meetings, and parent-teacher conferences, as well as preparing special props and materials for class. Taking a moment to place yourself in the teacher's shoes may help you better understand the responsibilities that an educator bears on a daily basis.

By now your child has attained a comfort level with teachers. Your fourth grader understands basic classroom rules and expectations, and finds himself enjoying a teacher who uses creative teaching methods to expose him to new and different experiences. The fourth grade teacher is often very imaginative, using a wide array of media to instruct and enthrall the class. Don't be surprised to hear your child chatter excitedly about a slide show or videotape shown during class to enhance a topic being covered in class.

THE EDUCATIONAL TEAM

YOUR child's educational team consists of many players. First and foremost are you and your fourth grader. Each of you have specific roles within the team. Just as a quarterback on a football team, it is up to you to be sure that the game plan is being followed. You will want to keep in tune with your child, and in touch with the other members of the educational team—your child's teachers. Other members of your child's educational team could include any teachers that your child interacts with throughout the school year, the school administrators, guidance counselors, and any other special instructors or teachers with whom your child interacts. Now that we have described the members of the team, and have given you a rough view of the playing field and conditions, we should jump in and start learning!

Parental involvement is one of the most critical aspects of a child's success in school. The school and parents must develop a relationship that consists of a mutual trust. It is of utmost importance that these two work cooperatively, especially as the child moves through the middle grades. The child, at this time, goes through so many physical and emotional changes and parents often do not know the impact that has on academics. This is the time that parents can work with the school to make sure all the child's needs are being met.

—An elementary school principal from Pennsylvania

How to Use This Book

Every child is unique, and therefore will require an education somewhat tailored to their learning style, special gifts, talents, and abilities. While it is important to be sensitive to your child's gifts, remember that all fourth graders are very similar in their social and intellectual growth. While we will touch on the traits that may make your child unique, this book will outline the abilities and capabilities of the average fourth grade student. We will discuss the average fourth grader's academic abilities, social growth, and special needs. Gaining a good baseline to the fourth grade persona, some tips to keep yourself and your child motivated, and some insider information on standardized tests will assist you in the important task of tailoring your child's educational experience to ensure his educational success.

Now that you have a basic overview of what to expect during this important year of fourth grade, you may ask, "How will this book further help me ensure my child's educational success?" This book is not meant to take the place of the natural instincts you possess. Only you know the special traits that make your fourth grader, and her special needs and talents, unique. Only you know if she is currently struggling academically or socially. While there are many resources available to parents that will stress the academic skills, and still others that give parents keen insight to a fourth grader's emotional state of being, this book is designed to describe both the academic and social milestones of the fourth grade. Understanding how these two facets of a child's growth work together will undoubtedly prove to be advantageous to all members of a child's educational team. Remember that you are a key member of that team. Working together with your child and his teachers will produce nothing but positive results.

During your initial read of this resource, you may find that some of the key points are not yet relevant to your child. Imagine, if you will, reading the owner's manual to your car. Initially you may peruse the manual, finding that not all of the features or instructions are immediately helpful, but as you drive the car for a period of time, you may find yourself referring to the manual to find important information. Use this book in the same manner. Read it initially to gain a baseline understanding of what to expect this year, then pick up the book throughout the year when you are faced with new questions or difficulties. By the end of the fourth grade, you may have a book with dog-eared pages, highlighted passages, and favorite nuggets of information.

2

What Your Child Is
Learning in School

AS MENTIONED in Chapter 1, fourth grade is commonly referred to as a transition year. This designation is often given to fourth grade because the subject matter becomes increasingly difficult over this school year and the students are expected to perform at a higher level, both academically and socially. Also, your fourth grader's increased independence could translate to his being less communicative about school or schoolwork. You may have to pry information from your fourth grader in an effort to keep in touch with what is being taught in the classroom. For all of these reasons, it is important that you find friendly, non-intimidating ways to involve yourself in your child's schoolwork. Taking a moment to peruse your child's textbooks, notebooks, and agenda or assignment book will give you a quick and accurate vision of the increased complexity of this year's curriculum. Spending these few minutes to familiarize yourself with the material your child is learning could keep you from being surprised if your child begins to struggle as the school year progresses. Having a clear idea of what your child is studying may inspire your imagination to find creative ways to support what is being taught at school during leisure and playtime at home.

WHAT REALLY HAPPENS IN FOURTH GRADE?

AS my children entered fourth grade, there was a lot of whispering by other parents—parents of older children. They surreptitiously would share information gleaned from their child's fourth grade experience. "This is a tough year, it makes or breaks 'em" was one line that a well-meaning parent shared with me. Yes, this sort of "advice" can be a bit unnerving to parents as their child heads off to the first day of fourth grade. Certainly a child's future is not completely altered by their performance in fourth grade, but this year your child will be introduced to subject matter and assignments that he has never encountered before. As the school year progresses, your fourth grader undoubtedly will be expected to complete individual projects, as well as some group assignments.

While fourth grade students continue to spend time with reading and language arts skills, these subjects will enter a maintenance phase—preventing the loss of the firm foundation created in the primary grades—especially in reading. The focus this year will be placed on science and social studies classes, as well as advancing math skills to include fractions and percentages. The four core subjects, Language Arts (Reading and Writing), Mathematics, Science, and Social Studies constitute the "Core Four." For more on the "Core Four," keep reading.

HOW IS THEIR TIME SPENT?

IN fourth grade the school day may seem a bit longer because fourth graders typically do not have as much recess or leisure time as they might have been accustomed to in earlier grades. Instead of recess time, students in the fourth grade may be introduced to social enrichment classes, such as computer and technology familiarization or life skills workshops. There may be a marked increase in your child's homework load, which is why your fourth grader's backpack will be heavy with notebooks and textbooks. A typical day for your fourth grader may be similar to the one shown below.

FOURTH GRADE CLASS SCHEDULE

8:45–9:15	Opening
9:15–10:00	Reading/Language Arts
10:00–10:20	Break
10:20–11:15	Mathematics
11:15–12:00	Rotating Subjects
12:00–12:30	Lunch
12:30–1:20	Social Studies
1:20–1:45	Writing
1:45–2:00	Read Aloud
2:00–2:30	Recess
2:30–3:10	Science
3:15	Dismissal

ROTATING SUBJECTS (11:15–12:00)

Monday:	Foreign Language
Tuesday:	Music
Wednesday:	Computer
Thursday:	Art
Friday:	Physical Education

The schedule above represents an average student, in an average school. It is understood that your child's schedule and class load may vary from the representative schedule.

Every day your child will spend almost six and a half hours at school learning, according to a report commissioned by the United States Department of Education. Slightly more than four of these six and a half hours will be spent concentrating on the Core Four.

➤ Almost 2 hours a day will be spent on Reading/Language Arts
➤ Approximately 1 hour a day will be spent working with Mathematics
➤ There will be 40 minutes a day devoted to Science
➤ Another 40 minutes a day will be devoted to Social Studies

Compared to third grade, the amount of time spent on Reading and Language Arts will decrease slightly this year, while the concentration on

Mathematics will remain constant. However, this school year will also include a marked increase in the amount of time and energy expended in the areas of Science and Social Studies. Although the actual increase in the time spent on these topics daily is nominal, the concentration will be more intense and focused. In Social Studies, your child may delve deep in our country's history, making models of popular forms of shelter in colonial America, giving oral reports on the type of person who may have lived in such a shelter, while also sharing and learning about the culture of early settlers.

Although your child may spend a little more or a little less time on each of the core subjects daily, you will be surprised to know that these numbers are surprisingly similar nationwide. Public schools may vary slightly from private schools in the amount of time spent on each subject; these variances are negligible though. According to a report published by the U.S. Department of Education, teaching strategies, environments, and materials may differ, but the time spent teaching our children core curriculum subjects remains relatively constant. After taking into account the time spent on the core four, the remaining two and a half hours of each school day will be spent on arts and athletic classes, transitional time (time spent between each class), and administrative time such as morning announcements and afternoon dismissal. Although every school has its own curriculum, or education action plan, the common fourth grade action plan includes instruction in Language Arts (Reading and Writing), Math, Science, and Social Studies. You may notice that your child is expected to perform in all disciplines across the curriculum. A social studies essay may be graded on spelling and grammar,

SIZE DOES MATTER

"Reducing class size is one of the most important investments we can make in our children's future," said President Bill Clinton. As a result, in 1999 Congress approved a $1.2 billion payment toward the president's effort to reduce the teacher-student ratio. In 2000, an additional $450 million was offered so that a total of nearly 50,000 teachers could be hired through the Federal Class-Size Reduction Program. Inspired by federal support, almost half the states in the union have made an effort to reduce class size, and therefore to improve the quality of education. As a testament to its success, schools that were able to hire more teachers with Class-Size Reduction funds have reduced the average number of students in each classroom from 23 students to 18 students.

From "The Class-Size Reduction Report"
September 2000,
by the U.S. Department of Education

for instance. Additional minor courses of study may be included in the fourth grade curriculum. These minor classes could include music, computer, art, physical education, and foreign language classes.

LEARNING THE LANGUAGE OF EDUCATION

HAVE you ever read a school handbook, attended a School Board meeting, or read an article discussing school reforms and policies? If you have, then you have undoubtedly come across words and phrases that were unfamiliar and foreign to you. Topics such as curriculum, core subjects, standardized testing (covered in Chapter 4), and special education, are commonly discussed, but often without clear definition. Gaining an understanding of the terminology of education, as well as the implementation of educational philosophies will further enable you, the parent, to be an active and effective member of your child's educational team. As you read this guide, you will grow more and more familiar with the language of education.

Fourth grade curriculums are different from the first three primary grades—they are more intensive. The teachers are preparing them step by step for the middle school years. At our school, each subject is integrated into the next. For example, spelling words are pertinent to their social studies and science classes. Math is part of all subjects, too.

—A PARENT FROM CHICAGO

THE CORE FOUR

UNDERSTANDING what your child is going to be learning this year allows you to better prepare yourself mentally for the tasks ahead. Just as you may study an itinerary or road map before a trip, studying a curriculum will help you become familiar with the educational journey your child is embarking on this year.

Language Arts

Reading

Most likely, your child already has gained many of the skills necessary for proficient reading and writing. Throughout his young educational career, there has been a focus on reading and understanding what has been read. You may recall that during the third grade school year, your child's focus turned from "learning to read" to "reading to learn." During the fourth grade school year, reading will become even more important. While your fourth grader will not spend as much time on formal reading instruction, a lot of time will be spent learning by reading textbooks, classroom handouts, and other resource materials. Some of the advanced reading skills that your child will learn are listed below.

➤ BUILD UPON EXISTING VOCABULARY

Your fourth grader will spend a lot of time with words. He will be reading new material, getting exposed to unfamiliar words, and storing those words away for future use. As he learns new words, he will also store a definition with that word, learn how to use it in context, and how that word relates to others words already stored in his vast vocabulary database.

➤ IMPROVE READING COMPREHENSION

Understanding what is being read is key to the success of the fourth grade student. Throughout the year comprehension skills will be honed using "tricks," such as making mental pictures, and predicting outcomes using context clues.

➤ RECOGNIZE VARIOUS TYPES OF LITERATURE, WELL-KNOWN AUTHORS, AND READ WITH UNDERSTANDING

Reading becomes more of a leisure activity for your fourth grader as she begins to choose favorite authors, genres, and writing styles.

➤ IDENTIFY THE ELEMENTS OF A STORY STRUCTURE

The fourth grade student will possess the ability to analyze a story by the end of the year. Through this analysis, he will detect and identify the theme, characters, setting, and plot, as well as the main idea that the author is trying to convey to the reader.

➤ PREDICT OUTCOME AND DRAW CONCLUSIONS

After reading a passage or portion of a larger piece of work, the fourth grade student will create and invent her own ideas of "what happened next."

➤ IDENTIFY CAUSE AND EFFECT RELATIONSHIPS

While analyzing and discussing a written work, your fourth grader will begin to see how each element within the story relates to other elements of the story, thus being able to correctly identify cause and effect relationships.

➤ MAKE DISTINCTIONS BETWEEN REALITY AND FANTASY, FACT AND OPINION

By the fourth grade, children are expected to have a vivid imagination, but should be able to separate the imaginary from the real. This translates to the material that they read as well. She should be able to conclude if a story is reality or fantasy, factual in nature, or a story grown from one's own opinions.

➤ PUT PARTS OF A STORY INTO CORRECT SEQUENCE

If given several portions of a complete story, in either word or picture format, the average fourth grader should possess the ability to place these portions into correct logical order.

➤ DEVELOP AN APPRECIATION AND LOVE OF READING

Most children who are supplied with a good learning environment, and are surrounded by those who love to read and champion reading as an enjoyable activity, will develop an appreciation of reading that will last a lifetime.

Writing

One aspect of the Reading/Language Arts course of study is writing. The fourth grade student will often use paper and pencil to convey ideas, questions, and solutions. Across the curriculum, the fourth grader will convey his ideas, solutions, and facts in written format. Essay questions will begin to appear on your child's science and social studies tests, mathematical equations may need to be converted to real-life word problems; this makes the fourth grader a student of many words. Fortunately, revising is becoming easier for the fourth grade writer. He is no longer so attached to his work that he resists removing unnecessary words or sentences. He will work toward a better-finished product. The fourth grade writer overflows with creativity. Descriptive writing is common as students learn to use adjectives and adverbs to better describe the setting of a story. Some of the key lessons learned in writing are as follows.

➤ USE THE WRITING PROCESS EFFECTIVELY

The fourth grade student is expected to follow a certain process to attain quality written works.

- Prewriting
- Drafting
- Peer sharing
- Revising
- Checking work

➤ IDENTIFY AND USE A VARIETY OF WRITING STYLES

The fourth grade child will be expected to write passages using the narrative, persuasive, and expository styles of writing.

Narrative: This style of writing is often found in fictional works. It describes and develops settings and characters.

Persuasive: This style of writing can be found in editorial writings, where the writer is trying to convince or sway the reader.

Expository: This style of writing is commonly found in textbooks or news media, where conveying facts in an unbiased manner is important.

➤ UNDERSTAND SENTENCE STRUCTURE, GRAMMATICAL STRUCTURE, NOUNS, VERBS, AND VERB TENSES

As your child becomes more exposed to the English language through reading and writing, as well as through classroom instruction, he will become more adept at understanding the parts of a sentence and how they are put together to create sentences.

➤ APPLY RULES OF CAPITALIZATION AND PUNCTUATION

The fourth grade student is expected to capitalize and punctuate correctly.

➤ DEVELOP PUBLIC SPEAKING SKILLS AND CRITICAL LISTENING SKILLS

Oral reports and discussion will encourage the fourth grade child to hone his public speaking skills.

➤ LEARN TO USE A DICTIONARY AND OTHER REFERENCE MATERIALS

Because fourth grade is rich in research and exposure to new research resources, the fourth grade student will gain confidence and knowledge in choosing not only which type of research resource will work best for a given problem, but also how to use the chosen resource correctly. Reference materials will include a dictionary, a thesaurus, encyclopedias, and the Internet.

➤ USE CORRECT SPELLING

Spelling differs from vocabulary, in that vocabulary refers to the understanding of a word, and its uses, whereas spelling refers to the ability to correctly use the letters of the alphabet to create that word. Often spelling and vocabulary are taught simultaneously, even using the same workbooks. Spelling is usually covered in a regimented process. The fourth grade student may be assigned new spelling words at the beginning of each week. The schedule below is a common spelling schedule.

Monday: Introduce new words
Tuesday: Take pretest plus spelling homework is assigned
Wednesday: Review spelling words plus spelling homework
    is assigned
Thursday: Take second pretest
Friday: Weekly spelling test

Often spelling lists will follow a particular theme, such as homophones or words that end in —ure. Here are some examples:

tail	measure
tale	pleasure
pain	treasure
pane	fracture
waist	future
waste	nature
wait	capture
weight	pasture
peace	culture
piece	moisture

Mathematics

The second subject of the Core Four is Mathematics. Numbers and numerical exercises are fun for some children, as they learn to manipulate them to solve their own problems. Other children will struggle, unable to form the correlation between the numerals represented on a piece of paper before them, and the physical entities they represent. Because basic addition and subtraction usually have been mastered by fourth grade, some advanced concepts are being introduced in math class this year. Your fourth grader may work with fractions and decimals, as well as performing multiplication and division functions on much larger numbers. An overview of the mathematics topics covered includes:

➤ PROBLEM SOLVING

Solving problems requires that a child first decide which operation should be used to obtain the correct solution: addition, subtraction, multiplication, or division.

➤ ESTIMATION

The fourth grade child should be able to:

■ Estimate numbers to thousands place
■ Round whole numbers to nearest 10, 100, and 1,000
■ Round money to nearest 10¢, $1, $10, and $100

The fourth grader should also be able to arrive at approximate sums, differences, products, and quotients by rounding.

➤ NUMBERS

Fourth graders will learn the place value system for numbers up to one million. He should also be able to read and write numbers to 999,999,999. Also, your child will know and understand number place value through millions. Children will also understand and identify prime numbers.

➤ ADDITION AND SUBTRACTION OF WHOLE NUMBERS

While your fourth grader has been adding and subtracting for several years, his math skills will increase this year. He will be expected to demonstrate a level of proficiency adding and subtracting 5-digit numbers.

Addition of 5 digit numbers $\quad 57,486 + 38,715 = ?$
Subtraction of 5 digit numbers $\quad 63,587 - 14,572 = ?$

➤ MULTIPLICATION OF WHOLE NUMBERS

During the third grade year, students became exposed to multiplication. A lot of time will be spent honing these multiplication skills. Your fourth grader will be completing problems this year requiring several levels of proficiency. Your fourth grader will work with these combinations:

4 digit by 1 digit	$1,254 \times 5 = ?$
2 digit by 2 digits	$63 \times 15 = ?$
3 digit by 2 digits	$418 \times 24 = ?$

➤ DIVISION OF WHOLE NUMBERS

After learning multiplication skills, students learn division. The fourth grade student will learn simple division skills such as:

Dividing by 1 digit divisors	$32 \div 8 = ?$
Zeroes in quotients	$50 \div 5 = ?$
Dividing by 2 digit divisors	
1 digit quotients	$100 \div 25 = ?$
2 digit quotients	$120 \div 11 = ?$
with remainders	

➤ DECIMALS

Although decimals are simply alternate representatives of fractions, children may have difficulty comprehending them. Fourth graders will learn many commonly used decimals as well as the fractional equivalent of that decimal. She then will be expected to perform basic mathematical operations accordingly.

➤ FRACTIONS

The fourth grade math student will understand and be able to manipulate fractions, as well as have the ability to present visual and decimal representations of a fractional number, and perform addition and subtraction of fractions (same denominator). The student will be expected to convert remainders in division into fractions. He will also learn to change fractions to whole numbers.

➤ MEASUREMENT

Using rulers and yardsticks, the fourth grade student will learn to measure almost anything and everything to the closest quarter or eighth of an inch. Your fourth grader will use both metric and standard units of measure to perform experiments that require both exact and estimated solutions. The student will learn to plug these measurements into formulas to figure perimeter and area.

➤ PERFORM BASIC MATH FUNCTIONS INCLUDING THE ELEMENTS OF TIME AND MONEY

This year there are new problems that involve time or money calculations. Your child may be asked to find solutions to problems that will have her figuring elapsed time or how much change is due a customer. These problems could be presented in the form of word problems or as visual representations.

➤ ORGANIZE AND INTERPRET MATERIALS ON GRAPHS AND CHARTS

Charts and graphs are commonplace in the fourth grade classroom. The fourth grade student enjoys interpreting what each chart and graph is trying to tell him. By the end of the year, the fourth grade student will be adept at creating simple charts and graphs to convey information.

➤ UNDERSTAND BASIC GEOMETRIC TERMS

Fourth grade students will have a good working knowledge of geometric terms such as polygon, angle, and diameter. The fourth grader also knows many geometric shapes and the properties that define them.

➤ APPLY KNOWLEDGE OF MATH PRINCIPLES IN REAL-WORLD APPLICATIONS INCLUDING "NON-MATHEMATICAL" ACTIVITIES

Whereas students in prior grades may have only practiced mathematical thinking during math class, the fourth grader will learn to use math in all aspects of his daily thinking. Your fourth grade little leaguer will use basic geometry skills to subconsciously figure the trajectory of a fly ball. While shopping, your fourth grader may estimate how many pieces of candy can be bought with her allowance.

➤ TRANSLATE NUMBERS INTO WORD PROBLEMS

Using a mathematical equation, your child will be able to create a story or word problem to correlate with the numbers and solutions already known.

➤ COLLECT, ANALYZE, AND MAKE SENSE OF REAL-WORLD DATA

It is not uncommon for the fourth grader to make a list of fruits and then poll each member in the classroom to find out each child's favorite fruit. The child can then give a summary of the fruits that the children in the classroom prefer, and can sort or group the answers according to popularity or other criteria.

➤ PRESENT DATA IN GRAPHICAL FORMS AND INTERPRET DATA GIVEN IN GRAPHICAL FORMS

Fourth graders will possess the ability to create circle and bar graphs to visually represent data that he is given or that he collects.

➤ IDENTIFY AND DEVELOP THE USE OF MATHEMATICAL SITUATIONS IN SCIENCE AND SOCIAL STUDIES

Your fourth grader will find that he is beginning to use math across the curriculum. He will use math skills in science and social studies as he takes measurements, interprets graphs, analyzes tables, and gains map skills.

➤ IDENTIFY NUMBERS AND EXTEND NUMBER PATTERNS, COMPARE NUMBERS, AND DEMONSTRATE NUMBER RELATIONSHIPS

Manipulating numbers with ease, identifying number patterns, and understanding relationships between numbers lays the groundwork for greater understanding of advanced mathematics.

Science

This year's classes will begin to feed the mad scientist hidden within your fourth grader. Throughout her elementary career, she has been exposed to science, but usually on a very superficial level. She has learned a bit about the world around her; about clouds and weather. She knows the planets, stars, and moon exist, and has a relatively good idea how they all revolve around the sun. This year's science class is going to dig a bit deeper. In the fourth grade students are given the opportunity to experience many different areas of the science disciplines. Physical science, life science, and earth science are all included in fourth grade studies. This year your child will be given the opportunity to get dirty, touch, and feel physical examples of scientific fact and theory. It is not uncommon for fourth grade science classes to visit environmental examples of the theories being taught in class. In the suburbs or rural schools, children may hop into hip-waders and visit a local stream, collecting information for experiments to be performed in the classroom. Urban school children may visit a playground or local factory to research scientific theories. Class trips to natural history museums and the like will be more substantive. Overall, this is a year of getting "into" science. This year's science student will learn many basic science facts and research skills.

➤ DEMONSTRATE THE SKILLS TO HYPOTHESIZE ABOUT SCIENTIFIC EXPERIMENTS

Fourth graders will be encouraged to think creatively and logically to predict the outcome of an experiment prior to actually performing the experiment or test.

➤ DEVELOP SCIENTIFIC PROCESSING SKILLS USED IN EXPERIMENTATION

Chances are that prior to performing any scientific experiment, your child will be instructed on documentation expectations, the technique to be used, and the amount of detail expected. All of these elements combine to create a scientific process.

➤ UNDERSTAND CONCEPTS IN LIFE SCIENCE

Through the study of flowering plants, animal behavior, food chains and food webs, and animal plant adaptations, your child will begin to have a greater understanding of the world around him, an appreciation for nature, and a beginner's look at life science.

➤ UNDERSTAND CONCEPTS IN PHYSICAL SCIENCE

Through the study of work, energy, electricity, magnetism, light, and sound, your fourth grader will be exposed to physical science theory.

➤ UNDERSTAND CONCEPTS IN EARTH SCIENCE

Through the study of changes in landforms, oceans, measuring weather conditions, and movement in the solar system, students will learn a bit about earth science.

➤ UNDERSTAND SOLAR PRINCIPLES

If your fourth grader is not already aware, he will discover that the earth rotates on its axis as it revolves around the primary source of energy for all living things; the sun.

➤ UNDERSTAND AND EXPLAIN THE FORMS OF MATTER

Fourth grade students will experience lessons in chemistry as they learn about the three forms of matter: liquid, solid, and gas.

➤ STUDY CELLS AND LIVING ORGANISMS

Students will be introduced to biology as they learn about simple cell structure and the fact that all living creatures are composed of cells.

The following skills may be taught either in conjunction with science or physical education (which is covered later in this chapter).

➤ LEARN ABOUT THE HUMAN BODY

Students will gain an understanding of the various systems that make up the human body and how they work together.

➤ LEARN GOOD DENTAL HYGIENE

Fourth graders will become familiar with the various types of teeth and the different attributes of each type. They will also learn good dental care and hygiene.

➤ LEARN HOW TO AVOID ADVERSE SITUATIONS

Your child will learn and practice good safety habits. Fourth graders will understand how to identify and avoid dangerous or difficult situations and how to avoid or react to these uncomfortable and possibly dangerous situations, such as unwanted attention from strangers.

➤ IDENTIFY GOOD NUTRITIONAL PRACTICES

Your child will become familiar with the food pyramid, each of the food groups, and which foods belong to each of the groups. Students will also learn about basic nutrition labels, and some keys to decoding these labels, to judge the nutritional qualities of a given food item.

➤ DIFFERENTIATE BETWEEN LEGAL AND ILLEGAL DRUGS

Your child may be involved in preliminary discussions about drugs. Assemblies and the "Just Say No" message are often touched upon, even during these young years. There may be discussion about responsible use of prescription drugs, and also, about the effects of recreational drug abuse. This preliminary and basic discussion may offer skills and techniques to avoid the taking of illegal drugs. This topic, as well as peer pressure, is discussed more in depth in Chapter 5.

Social Studies

Social Studies is one of the Core Four that increases in focus in fourth grade.

➤ GAIN AN UNDERSTANDING OF WORLD GEOGRAPHY

Fourth graders should be familiar with finding and identifying the continents and oceans on any standard map or globe. This will be easy for students because the classrooms and textbooks of fourth graders are usually plentiful with maps.

➤ HAVE A WORKING KNOWLEDGE OF MAPS

Because the fourth grade classroom is often filled with maps, charts, atlases, and globes, longitude and latitude, directions, and topography are all terms and concepts with which your fourth grader will become familiar.

➤ UNDERSTAND GEOGRAPHICAL RELATIONSHIPS

Using the new knowledge of maps and map-related terms and concepts, the fourth grade student will learn to describe the relationships between two points using cardinal directions (north, south, east, west), descriptions of hemisphere, or latitude and longitude descriptions.

➤ DEVELOP AN UNDERSTANDING OF EARLY CIVILIZATIONS

Utilizing available evidence and artifacts, students will gain insight to the living conditions of Native and Early Americans.

➤ UNDERSTAND EARLY AMERICAN CONFLICTS

Students will be familiarized with the conflicts that occurred between Native Americans and the migrating Europeans. Major milestones of the American Revolution and Civil War also will be discussed, and the student will gain a full understanding of the events surrounding these two major conflicts. The students will gain a basic understanding of how these conflicts affected the growing nation.

➤ DISCUSS CURRENT EVENTS ON A LOCAL, NATIONAL, AND GLOBAL SCALE

Your fourth grader may listen to the news, ask questions about an upcoming election, or discuss a global environmental concern. Some of this new curiosity can be attributed to school, where discussions about current events are not uncommon. Some media products have been introduced specifically for keeping children abreast of current events. You may recognize magazines such as *Time for Kids*, *Sports Illustrated for Kids*, or websites like *Yahooligans.com* or *CNN.com*, which have stories to stimulate the minds of young children. Also commonly used in the classroom are *Weekly Reader* handouts, which cover a variety of intellectually stimulating topics, including current events.

➤ UNDERSTAND LOCAL GOVERNMENT

Fourth graders will become familiar with local government, often using specialized materials created by the school district or another local source.

➤ BE FAMILIAR WITH IMPORTANT HISTORICAL FIGURES

Important historical figures, both local and national, will be introduced. Your child may be expected to write a report or do a project on a favorite historical person.

➤ UNDERSTAND RECYCLING AND ENVIRONMENTAL ISSUES

Throughout your child's school career, the effects of humans on the environment will be discussed. Your child will become acutely aware of the effects of recycling, reusing, and conservation.

➤ DISCUSS THE QUALITIES OF GOOD CITIZENSHIP

Students will learn some of the qualities of a good citizen, such as allegiance and civil service.

➤ UNDERSTAND THE THREE BRANCHES AND LEVELS OF GOVERNMENT

Students will learn about the three branches of federal government, which includes the executive, legislative, and judicial branches. In addition, the three levels of government (national, state, and local) will be briefly discussed.

ROTATING SUBJECTS

THROUGHOUT the week, your fourth grader will attend classes that cover subjects such as Music, Library, Art, Foreign Language and Physical Education. A typical fourth grade schedule includes at least one of these classes per day.

Library, Music, Foreign Language and Art classes often occur once a week, while many schools require that Physical Education classes be offered twice a week. These classes are familiar to your fourth grader, as she has been participating in them for most of her elementary school career. A teacher within the school system who has specialized training usually instructs these classes. Children of all grades enjoy these classes immensely, probably because they give the child a change of pace, change of scenery, and change of teacher in their day.

These special classes also provide enrichment to your child's education. Enrichment can best be described as the broadening of horizons. While your child is learning the basics of education by studying the core four, the special classes in arts and athletics expose the fourth grade student to subjects, theories, and arts that may not be readily available at home or in the conventional classroom setting.

This year, some of the arts and athletics classes will become a bit more difficult. While the younger student learned how to paint or create rudimentary sculpting, the fourth grade student may begin to learn the names of various painting or sculpting techniques. In music, the student may begin to learn about some of the famous musicians of the past, learning not only theory, but also history.

Foreign Language

Not all schools offer a foreign language in the elementary years, but if yours does, your fourth grader may cover the following information this year. According to a report distributed by the U.S. Department of Education, over the past decade, the number of elementary schools offering foreign language instruction increased by nearly 10%, from 22% to 31% of all elementary schools. These numbers show no signs of decreasing. If you are concerned about your child's proficiency at foreign language classes, know that the primary goal of most elementary school foreign language programs is to provide introductory exposure to the students. Only 21% of the participating elementary schools offer programs where language proficiency is a goal. In the introductory programs, the fourth grade foreign-language student will:

➤ begin to utilize textbooks to extend skills with the written, as well as spoken, language.

➤ extend vocabulary to include food, descriptive words, and professions.

➤ extend grammar to include future actions, adjectives, pronouns, and contractions.

➤ explore cultural understanding through individual reports and presentations.

➤ extend student written work in Spanish with basic vocabulary and sentence structures.

Music

Music is an important part of culture and history. Throughout the ages, music has been associated with celebration, victories, grieving, and sadness. This year, your child will gain more in-depth musical knowledge, such as learning to recognize musical notations, various musical styles, and how they relate to events in history. Children in fourth grade are often given the opportunity to learn to play a musical instrument and become members of the elementary band. To build on a child's musical knowledge, private or small group lessons may be offered to students who have chosen to learn to play an instrument. Other students may become members of the elementary chorus. These students may meet weekly for voice training and performing skill instruction. Provided your child's school has funds, children in fourth grade may be given the opportunity to learn basic music in a weekly class. With the skills taught in these classes, a student may learn to:

➤ Recognize different beat organizations and patterns

➤ Use notation for quarter, eighth, and sixteenth notes

➤ Recognize phrase length and content and whether its cadences are weak or strong

➤ Explore operatic style

➤ Explore musical theater style

➤ Basic knowledge of note-reading, instrument identification, music terms

Library

When your child mentions his visits to the school library, you may remember the shelves upon shelves of books, catalogued and categorized for ease of location. Today's library is not so different. Libraries still contain a huge variety of books, covering a multitude of topics, and representing many genres. The school library is usually centrally located. Students from all grades will visit the library and choose books for both leisure and research. The fourth grade student will usually stride confidently into the school library, already familiar with the lay of the land, so to speak. Your child will build upon her basic library research skills, becoming even more familiar with some of the resources available.

Your fourth grader is already familiar with the anatomy of a book, and is able to efficiently locate such information as the author, publisher, and year of publication within a book. This year she will become more familiar with the techniques used to categorize these books. If it has not already been covered in the lower grades, the Dewey Decimal System will be introduced.

Information in today's library is not only stored in books, but also as digital files, microfiche, and other sources. Your fourth grader will learn how to find all types and genres of information in the library. The complete collection of information stored in a library is often called "media." For that reason, your child's library may be referred to as the Media Center. To familiarize your child with the wide range of media available to her, search techniques will be introduced, explored, and discussed. The card catalog, whether physical or digital, will become an essential part of your child's library experience. Using either the electronic or traditional card catalog, your fourth grader will search for books or other forms of media according to title or author. Some of the skills your fourth grader will learn include the ability to:

➤ LOCATE, RETRIEVE, AND HANDLE
MEDIA AND EQUIPMENT

Your fourth grader should be able to identify symbols in the library media center and become familiar with the layout of the library. Using this information, your child will be able to obtain information using a variety of sources. Some of the basic methods of information retrieval are the card catalog and Dewey Decimal System.

➤ SELECT AND EVALUATE MEDIA

The fourth grader will begin to appreciate the resources available to her in the school library. When doing schoolwork, she will identify the need for information and then select and use appropriate materials.

➤ ORGANIZE AND MANAGE INFORMATION

After your fourth grader recognizes his need for information, he will require the ability to identify and use a variety of reference sources to locate the information he desires. He will use research techniques to locate information, as well as to create and organize bibliographies.

➤ COMPREHEND CONTENT

Your fourth grader will expand on her ability to recognize the variety of material available in the library media center. After identifying the appropriate resources, she will be able to comprehend the context in which the resource was written, whether factual, editorial, or fiction.

➤ APPRECIATE MEDIA

As well as learning to use the library as a resource and research center, your fourth grader will choose reading as a major source of information and as a leisure time activity. He will select books and media from the library media center. He will learn to recognize authors and illustrators and their work as he explores a wide variety of literature. This appreciation will allow him to relate literary experiences to personal experiences.

Art

Some of the favorite items on my desk at the office are items created in art class by my children. There is the clay box created by my oldest, a foamy fish on a stick, with foam-like seaweed as a base, and the flowerpot filled with fake flowers with a recipe for a happy family displayed on an index card peeking out from the faux flowers. Chances are that your refrigerator, office wall, or desk is covered with works of art created by your mini-Michelangelo! Students usually remember the school art room long after their educational careers have ended. Perhaps this is because art class ranks among the favorites for most elementary school students. Even children who are not particularly gifted enjoy the creative environment of art class. Unaware of methods and styles being taught to them, they revel in using paints, clay, and paste to create their own masterpieces. Fourth graders will learn the role and association of various types of art as it pertains to history. He may recognize a piece of art that could be associated with the Revolutionary War, or another piece that could best be attributed to a particular artist. Therefore, a student not only learns how to create art, but also the people, history, and styles associated with art through the ages. During this year, your fourth grader may learn to:

- ➤ Discuss the elements of composition
- ➤ Identify related and complementary colors
- ➤ Discuss texture in art media and the environment
- ➤ Create an art composition which conveys a sense of balance
- ➤ Create pictures with foreground and background
- ➤ Create a clay relief object
- ➤ Participate in the development of a mural
- ➤ Mount a painting
- ➤ Create a point of emphasis by using contrasting colors
- ➤ Recognize and discuss additional techniques used to create dimension
- ➤ Examine and discuss additional works of art
- ➤ Expand understanding and use of artistic terms
- ➤ Assume responsibility for care of art materials

Physical Education

Some children think of gym class as an added recess placed into the schedule a few days of the week. To other children, physical education class is an event that is met with much trepidation. For both groups of groups of children, there is the absence of realization that there is indeed purpose behind this organized play. Your child is refining both fine and large motor skills, and is gaining the ability to connect his mental and physical self successfully.

Your child is gaining knowledge and appreciation of the benefits of a healthy lifestyle. He will learn to exercise regularly, both independently, or in group activities. He will also learn some basic life skills such as following rules, teamwork, and good sportsmanship. Some of the games and activities played in fourth grade physical education classes are:

➤ Group games
➤ Manipulative activities: Frisbee, beanbag, parachute
➤ Individual activities
➤ Presidential Physical Fitness Test
➤ Track: running races, softball throw
➤ Volleyball: skills, rules, and strategy
➤ Basketball: skills, rules, and strategy
➤ Hockey: skills, rules, and strategy
➤ Soccer: skills, rules, and strategy
➤ Flag football: skills, rules, and strategy
➤ Softball or wiffle ball: skills, rules, and strategy
➤ Dance
➤ Gymnastics

Your fourth grader may be physically tested using the Presidential Physical Fitness Program. The Presidential Physical Fitness Program was created to encourage healthy lifestyles, exercise and achievement in children. For over thirty years children nationwide have been participating in the program. The Presidential Fitness Program includes the following activities:

➤ Curl Ups—To measure abdominal strength/endurance by maximum number of curl-ups performed in one minute
➤ Shuttle Run—To perform the shuttle run as fast as possible
➤ Distance Run/Walk—To measure heart/lung endurance by fastest time to run a long distance
➤ Pull-Ups—To measure upper body strength/endurance by maximum number of pull-ups completed
➤ Sit and Reach—To measure flexibility of lower back and hamstrings by reaching forward in the forward reach position

Children who perform these physical activities with the levels of proficiency show below are presented with an award; The Presidential Physical Fitness Award.

Boys Qualifying Standards are:

AGE	SHUTTLE RUN	CURL UPS	SIT / REACH	PULL-UPS	600 YARDS
9	10.9	41	31	5	2:11
10	10.3	45	30	6	2:11

Girls Qualifying Standards are:

AGE	SHUTTLE RUN	CURL UPS	SIT / REACH	PULL-UPS	600 YARDS
9	11.1	39	33	2	2:30
10	10.8	40	33	3	2:30

Note that these standards do change. Be sure to check with your child's physical education instructor to find out the exact standards will be used to evaluate your child's physical fitness.

Computer

One of the major changes in elementary education over the past decade is the addition of information technology or basic computer skills classes to the curriculum. It is highly probable that your child's classroom will have at least one computer, perhaps tucked into the rear of the class. This computer often times will contain software used to enhance the lessons taught via conventional means such as through textbooks, worksheets, and films.

Children are becoming adept at using technology for productivity, administrative, and learning tasks. Your child may also attend a computer skills class throughout the week. This class may be held in a computer lab. Students attending these classes will gain a basic understanding of computers, their associated peripherals, and software applications. Skills gained could include basic word processing, productivity, and researching skills. Your fourth grader may also impress you as he displays his knowledge of some of the features and tools, such as spell check, found within basic software. In today's digital age, children who have access to computers have a head start on productivity as they advance to higher educational levels. While a majority of your child's computer class time will be spent learning basic keyboarding skills, he will also spend time learning basic computer terminology and some of the components that make up a computer. By the end of fourth grade, your child will probably be able to:

➤ Choose technology tools appropriate to the task
➤ Recognize relationships of hardware and peripherals
➤ Understand and follow directions using basic technology
➤ Know, understand, and follow school rules related to technology
➤ Identify and assume roles to facilitate working collaboratively
➤ Examine how computers store, process, and retrieve information
➤ Identify and profile people who work at jobs that involve computers and technology
➤ Discuss the consequences of using technology in an inappropriate manner

Do not become intimidated by your child's computer prowess. Instead use this knowledge to initiate discussion and some valuable quality time. If you are uncomfortable with technology, let your child teach you some basic skills. It will not only benefit you, but it will certainly boost her self-esteem to be the teacher.

THE INVISIBLE CURRICULUM

WE have covered the Core Four, as well as the special subjects that are often offered in fourth grade, but your child will be learning other lessons this year. Because this is a transition year, your fourth grader will need to learn some new organizational skills to succeed. Although your child's teachers may not have documented these skills, they are the unwritten rules and skills that all teachers encourage in their students, and can be referred to as "The Invisible Curriculum." Your fourth grader will get a lot of practice using the skills learned in the invisible curriculum as he winds his way through the halls of fourth grade. Skills taught in the invisible curriculum include the ability to:

➤ Develop skill in task definition (What do I know? How do I find out?)
➤ Differentiate between relevant and irrelevant information
➤ Learn a variety of note taking strategies (webbing, lists, charts, mapping, two-column notes, what I: know, want to know, have learned)
➤ Identify and restate main ideas and key points
➤ Use reference materials needed to find specific information
➤ Use information to problem solve
➤ Demonstrate self-organization (assignment books, homework, supplies)
➤ Use class and school library to access information

Fourth grade children also learn valuable lessons in teamwork. It is common for teachers to assign group projects in fourth grade, whether it is a classroom bulletin board, or a formal report, children will be placed in teams. Using some of the other skills learned in the invisible curriculum, children will organize themselves and learn to work together to reach a common goal.

SUMMARY

AS you can see, this year really is a unique, transitional year for your fourth grader. Your child will be very busy learning both the standard and the invisible curriculum. Your child will begin to choose certain classes as "favorites." She may especially enjoy math class, or perhaps social studies is her love. Be prepared though, because some children, even those who have previously exhibited no signs of difficulty, may experience some growing pains or difficulties with the more advanced nature of this year's schoolwork. Your fourth grader may struggle with organizational skills, but will probably be able to prioritize and organize herself to an acceptable degree by the end of this school year.

3

How to Supplement What Your Child Is Learning

PREPARING your child for the future is the goal of your fourth grader's educational team. Whether or not you are an active participant, you *are* a member of your child's educational team. Your membership in this important team carries some weighty responsibilities. Just as a football or baseball team performs best when all team members work toward a common goal, your educational team will thrive with willing participation from all members. By being an active team member, you are providing your child with countless tools—all of which will aid in the ultimate quest of educational success.

You might believe that you are not fully prepared to be an active participant on the educational team, but you could not be further from the truth. Although you might not know or understand the many details of your child's curriculum, you are armed with an incredible strength. This strength is your intimate knowledge of your child's personality. You know better than anyone else what makes your child tick, what interests they actively pursue in their playtime, and how he best learns new skills. Because of this invaluable knowledge, you are a very necessary member of the team. Also, your child mimics your behavior. Attitudes, habits, and values that you display will directly affect your fourth grader's attitude, habits, and value decisions. If you are excited about education and learning, chances are high that your child will be, too.

Understanding your child's school day gives you a good start to organizing and planning learning experiences at home. Throughout the day your fourth grader will be one of many students. On average, most fourth grade classrooms have approximately 22 to 25 students. It is also probable that your young student is changing classrooms and interacting with different teachers throughout the day; therefore, her day is spent in the company of many students, a variety of teachers, and in a collection of classrooms. Your child's special needs or talents become part of a patchwork of many children's special needs or talents, and are often not immediately recognizable to the other members of your fourth grader's educational team. On the other hand, your home and the members of your household are constants in her day. You provide an environment where your child is given the opportunity to be one of few—instead of one of many. Her needs and talents are sometimes more obvious to you than they are to her teachers because simply, you are able to provide her with more one-on-one attention. With this extra attention, your fourth grader will be able to further discuss favorite subjects, frustrating difficulties, and her broadening range of interests.

LET'S TALK ABOUT IT

I F your child has witnessed your enthusiasm to be involved in his education, he will enjoy sharing the day's events with you. If you are not genuinely enthused, or if you find a particular topic unexciting or difficult, try to show interest anyway. Your fourth grader's willingness to share may dissipate if he senses that you are not interested. That is why it is extremely important, in fact imperative, that you open these lines of communication—and keep them open.

Communicating about the day's events does not mean that you have to do all the talking or asking of questions. Set aside a particular time of the day when you and your child connect with one another. You may share some particularly interesting tidbits about your day, and your child may then share some interesting facts or events about his day. Pay particular attention not only to what he says, but also to what he does not say. You can learn a lot by merely giving your child the opportunity to talk. Does your child have a pattern of only discussing math and science, while never mentioning reading class? Perhaps he is avoiding a dialogue about reading because he does not like the subject, is uncomfortable with the content, or is having difficulties. He may be sharing information about math and science because he is most proud of those subjects. He may be excelling in those classes, or perhaps he is intrigued with the teacher's methods of presenting lessons to the class.

If you notice that your fourth grader is showing signs of frustration, do not be discouraged. You can help your child overcome this hurdle, and be better prepared for the next hurdle. One of the best techniques for helping a child over a rough spot is to jump in and help her understand and master the stubborn task at hand. If you find that the task is difficult for you as well, take heart. Your child will actually gain self-confidence and improve her sense of self as the two of you work toward finding solutions. Her sense of self-esteem will actually improve when she realizes that she is not alone in her frustrations.

BUT, I AM NOT QUALIFIED

JUST remember that being an involved and successful member of the educational team does not mandate that you have a college education, a high school diploma, or any mixture of educational experiences. You don't have to have strong skills in all subjects. You do not have to belong to any particular socio-economic group. In order to be a successful team member, you must only have the enthusiasm and drive necessary to encourage and help your child.

A strong support network of involved parents facilitates successful parental involvement in student studies and activities. Do not hesitate to turn to other parents when your child is experiencing academic difficulties. Often other parents have been in your shoes, and will be willing to brainstorm with you—helping to find solutions to your child's social or academic needs. Because other parents are often great sources of information and ideas, they often are the best source of fun activities to challenge and inspire children academically.

FIND YOUR SUPPORT NETWORK!

Become involved in your local Parent Teacher Association. Also visit the website at: *www.pta.org.* Discover online support networks at parenting and education websites such as: *www.parentsoup.com,* *www.parentsplace.com,* and *www.familyeducation.com.*

LEARNING STYLES

AMONG your fourth grader's friends, you have probably noticed a variety of personalities. There are some children who naturally take the lead and make decisions. Other children are more likely to follow the group, not making waves within the group. Some children are very active performers who entertain and amuse. Just as all of these children have very different personalities, so do they have very different learning styles.

A learning style is a method of perceiving and processing information. Think back to when your child was learning basic math facts. Which method of learning fit best? Did he write and re-write the facts until committed to memory, or did he say them aloud over and over, in an almost singsong fashion? Did your use of manipulatives and real life examples help etch the math facts indelibly into his memory? All are examples of how your child's learning style affected the way he studied and mastered his tasks. Having a keen understanding of your child's learning style(s) allows you to facilitate a learning environment tailored to his needs. Your child may have more than one learning style; in fact, it is most likely that your fourth grader will possess at least two distinct learning styles.

There are at least seven commonly recognized styles of learning. See if you can find your child's learning styles from the following specifications.

Physical

The child with a physical learning style is easily identified. You will notice them in a room, fidgeting, twisting their hair, and playing with their school supplies. Sitting still is a concept lost on these active children. It is best explained that these children think well while moving. Usually these children will enjoy sports, activities, and just plain "doing." They will enjoy acting out, interacting with manipulatives or teaching tools, and will enjoy any sort of dance or movement. Examples of adult physical learners are professional athletes, craftspersons, surgeons, actors, and dancers.

Intrapersonal

It is possible that unless you are an intrapersonal learner, you may have trouble remembering one that you went to school with. Often times the intrapersonal learner is described as shy or introverted. Intrapersonal learners are not antisocial; they simply think better when they are allowed to focus completely and independently. Sometimes they are described as reserved, which is not truly accurate. Although they do sometimes march to the beat of their own drum, they usually are just busy thinking and processing information. They prefer to do things alone, rather than as a large group. The intrapersonal learner excels when learning new information via self-paced activities or independent projects. Psychologists, philosophers, and computer programmers are all examples of careers where intrapersonal learners succeed.

I hear and I forget, I see and I remember, I do and I understand.

—CONFUCIUS

Interpersonal

Now that we know what intrapersonal learners are, it is not difficult to surmise what an interpersonal learner is. These children are often described as social butterflies. You will notice them while volunteering at your child's school. The interpersonal learner will be anxious to help others, raising their hand to help the teacher and fellow students with almost anything that will allow them the opportunity to interact with others. This type of learner will enjoy group activities, relishing the time spent sharing ideas. The interpersonal learner will cooperate well with others and will enjoy researching and performing tasks with small groups of people, rather than independently. Teachers, politicians, entertainers, and business executives often fall under this learning style.

Linguistic

The linguistic learner usually will have a wonderful vocabulary, and will use it in both written and spoken language. This child will almost always be accompanied by a book. Linguistic learners will enjoy giving speeches and oral reports almost as much as they enjoy reading and creative writing. Linguistic learners gain a lot of knowledge simply by listening to lectures and reading textbooks and anecdotes. Linguistic learners often grow to become authors, journalists, or lecturers.

Mathematical

Mathematical learners thrive in logic. These children understand and follow rules, almost too stringently. They have a keen understanding of mathematics, numbers, and patterns. The mathematical learner will enjoy brainteasers and math puzzles. This type of learner benefits most by experimenting and using statistics and calculations. Mathematical learners succeed in careers such as science, mathematics, accounting, and law.

Musical

Although this learning style tends to hint that a child with this learning style excels in music, that is not true. Simply, musical learners sing, hum, and feel musically. They hear and understand melodies in the world around them. Children who are musical learners will make up songs and ditties to help them remember and recall facts. They will thrive in environments where learning is accomplished with a variety of multimedia resources. Singers, musicians, and web designers are often musical learners.

Visual

Visual learners are doodlers and artists. They have a keen understanding of color and lines. Pictures, images, and art are appealing to these learners. The visual learner may enjoy painting, graphing, and creating maps. Drawing charts, creating diagrams, using colors and spatial relationships give understanding to the lessons they are learning. Visual learners often grow up to be architects, painters, and pilots.

Now that you have identified the learning style(s) that best suit your child, you possess the information that will allow you to proactively find the methodologies to best help your child on the path to educational success. If your child is struggling, refer to the learning style list to find some of the activity types that seem to work well with your child's style. After identifying those activity types, consult the following list to find activities that will give your child the best chance to perceive and process information.

GENERAL TIPS—ACROSS THE CURRICULUM

LEARNING occurs every day and everywhere, not just during the school year, or on the school campus. For this reason, you will want to find ways to encourage and supplement your child's learning at home. Later in the chapter we will discuss curriculum-specific methods of encouraging and engaging your child, however there are some tips and ideas that don't fit into just one subject. These tips will not only help your child across the entire fourth grade curriculum, but throughout life.

First and foremost, in every area of your life, be a good role model. Even as your fourth grader grows into adulthood, he will look to you for guidance. Never forget or discount the effect you have on your child. He will watch as you interact with others. He will listen to your speaking patterns. He will take great pride in your accomplishments. He will mimic your excitement, and may become sullen when you are angry or distant. Teach your child life skills; admit when you are wrong, volunteer in your community, be affectionate.

Recognize your child's learning style and personality. The learning styles listed in this chapter provide clues to successfully engaging your child in the educational process. Use these clues to your advantage. For example, do not force your child to study alone in his or her bedroom if the list suggests that your child is an interpersonal learner.

Involve your child in activities that fit his learning style and your schedule. Carefully choose an organization or two in which to enroll your fourth grader.

Perhaps the local YMCA or YWCA is offering workshops in something that your fourth grader has expressed interest in, or maybe your church offers a youth organization. Often these types of organizations will teach children valuable life skills that supplement conventional academics. In these types of organizations, your child may learn about volunteerism, science, safety, or hygiene. Usually these organizations and workshops are run by people who genuinely enjoy what they do, and create a fun learning environment outside of the pressures of school.

Most of all, make your involvement in your child's life a priority. Every child deserves to feel special. Your involvement gives your child that special feeling, while also teaching life lessons and ensuring educational success. The next section of this chapter provides parents with tips, ideas, and activities that can give them a jumpstart in supplementing their child's learning. Many of these activities also make for great quality time/bonding experiences for the parent and child.

READING/LANGUAGE ARTS

READING, or the task of learning to read, is less focused upon this year than any of the previous years. It's likely that your child is already reading chapter books, and sounds out and recognizes words proficiently. She is probably able to decipher new words using the surrounding words as context clues.

A mistake common among parents of proficient readers is that reading aloud is no longer important. A fourth grader is certainly capable of choosing and reading books that are of an appropriate reading level, and because of this parents believe that their role as reading partners has disappeared. Do not fall into this pattern. Although your child is a bit taller, a bit lankier, and possibly more difficult to fit on your lap or to share a cozy chair with, reading aloud is still something that your child will enjoy. Your fourth grader has only begun her reading journey. She will learn good reading techniques, inflection, and word decoding simply by spending fifteen minutes or so with you, each night, reading aloud to one another. The emotional benefits of reading with your child far surpass the academic benefits she will receive. The social and emotional well-being that spending quality time with a parent or loved one creates far exceeds any academic goals that you would like your child to reach.

Some General Tips

➤ Read aloud to your child: books, newspaper and magazine articles, the back of the cereal box, labels on cans, or directions.

➤ Read poems aloud together to learn about rhythm and repeated sounds in language.

➤ Establish a reading time, even if it's only ten minutes each day. Make sure there is a good reading light in your child's room and stock her bookshelves with books and magazines that are easy to both read and reach.

➤ Listen to your child read homework or favorite stories to you regularly.

➤ Go to the library together and check out books. Be sure to ask the librarian for good books or to help you locate resources.

➤ Have books, magazines, and papers around the house, and let your child see that reading is an important activity in your home.

➤ Encourage older children to read to younger children.

➤ Help experienced readers talk and write about what they read.

➤ Encourage activities that require reading. Cooking (reading a recipe), constructing a kite (reading directions), or identifying a bird's nest or a shell at the beach (reading a reference book) are some examples.

I have a nine year old who loves to read. And she also loves to be read to—and I'm just discovering this. I thought she had "outgrown" this because she knows how to read, but I was wrong.

—A PARENT AND TEACHER FROM TEXAS

Activities

And That's the End of the Story...

Improve listening skills and imagination. Read a story aloud to your child and stop before the end. Ask the child, "What do you think is going to happen next?" Then finish the story and discuss the ending with the child. Did it turn out the way you thought? This activity will expand and improve your child's imagination and reasoning skills.

Journal Writing

Encourage journal writing at home as well as at school. Provide your fourth grader with a notebook, pencils, and a quiet place where he can keep his thoughts. Be a good role model; why not take it a step further and start a journal yourself? Document your fourth grader's growth. Both journals will become treasured keepsakes for years to come.

Reading and Writing

1. Reading and writing go hand in hand. Have your child read school assignments aloud.
2. Explain that when you read, you should listen to how the writing sounds by asking yourself:

   - Does the writing sound the way people talk?
   - Is it smooth or choppy?
   - Are there any words or ideas missing?
   - How could the writing be made more interesting? By adding descriptions, using examples, or going into more detail with explanations?

3. Encourage your child to read with expression, emphasizing the words in the sentences that are most important to your child.
4. Encourage others who might be listening to ask questions about the writing.

MATH

THE fourth grade is the first year where numbers and math are greatly emphasized. The fourth grade student will begin to learn higher thinking skills as they pertain to numbers. Division, fractions, and decimals are all covered in fourth grade, and these skills can cause difficulties. You will want to find fun ways to show concrete examples of every day uses of mathematics skills. As soon as your fourth grader understands the reasons behind certain mathematical concepts, he will better understand them.

The U.S. Department of Education offers the following tips to parents who are helping their children achieve educational success in mathematics:

➤ Visit your child's school. Meet with your child's teacher to see if your child is actively involved in math. Find out how you can help your child to better understand math problems.

➤ Set high standards for your child in math. Make sure your child is mathematically challenged and encourage his or her interest and pursuit of math.

➤ Help children see that math is very much a part of everyday life. From statistics in sports to the sale price of clothing, from the calories in food to the amount of gas needed to travel from one city to another, math is important to us every day. Help your child make these connections to math.

➤ Point out that many jobs require math. From the scientist to the doctor, from the plant manager to the newspaper salesman, from the computer programmer to the hardware store owner, many jobs require a strong foundation in math. Help your child see that math leads to many exciting career opportunities.

➤ Stimulate your child's interest in technology. Encourage your child to use calculators and computers to further learning.

➤ Play games that help children develop decision-making and mental math skills. There are many games sold commercially, such as board games, that involve patterns and probability.

➤ Play games from your own family traditions such as counting games and games that keep score. Try schoolyard games such as jump rope, hopscotch, and jacks. Games require children to use strategies to make decisions, solve problems, and develop an understanding about numbers and how to use them (number sense) and computational skills.

➤ Positive attitudes about math will reinforce encouragement. Your feelings will have an impact on how your children think about math and themselves as mathematicians. Positive attitudes about math are important in encouraging your child to think mathematically.

➤ Show your children that you like numbers. Play number games and think of math problems as puzzles to be solved.

➤ Put things into groups. When you do laundry, separate items of clothing: all the socks in one pile, shirts in another, and pants in another. Divide the socks by color and count the number of each. Draw pictures and graphs of clothes in the laundry: 4 red socks, 10 blue socks, 12 white socks. Create graphs using the data collected.

➤ Reinforce to your children that anyone can learn math. Point out numbers in your child's life: in terms of weight, measurements involving cooking, temperature, and time.

➤ Help your children do math in their heads with lots of small numbers. Ask questions: "If I have 4 cups and I need 7, how many more do I need?" or "If I need 12 drinks for the class, how many packages of 3 drinks will I need?" Encourage speedy and accurate answers to these types of questions.

Activities

Total It

What you'll need: license plates, paper, pencil, and calculator.

As you are traveling in your car, or on a bus, each person takes turns calling out a license plate number. All players try to add the numbers in their heads. Talk about what strategies were used in the mental math addition. Were the numbers added by 10's like 2 + 8? Were doubles like 6 + 6 added? Try different problems using the numbers in a license plate. For example, if you use the plate number 663M218, ask "Using the numbers on the plate, can you make 5?"

➤ using two numbers? "Yes, 3 + 2 = 5"
➤ using three numbers? "Yes, (3 + 2) × 1 = 5"
➤ using four numbers? "Yes, (6 + 3 + 1) ÷ 2 = 5"
➤ using five numbers? "Yes, (6 + 6 + 3) − (8 + 2) = 5"
➤ using six numbers? "Yes, (6 + 6) + (3 × 1) − (8 + 2) = 5"

GREAT IDEA!

Ease on Down the Road

Driving your children from home, to school, to soccer practice racks up the miles on your car, but also provides ample opportunity to practice math skills. Try this:

A gallon of gas costs $1.52 a gallon. What does it cost for 5 gallons? 10 gallons? 15 gallons? 20 gallons? What is an easy way to figure this out? How can you estimate the cost by rounding the cost per gallon?

The speed limit is 55 miles per hour. How far will you go in 1 hour? Two hours? Three hours? How long will it take to go 500 miles?

Weighing In

What you'll need: A grocery scale or your scale at home.

Help your child examine the scale in the grocery store or the one you have at home. Explain that pounds are divided into smaller parts called ounces and 16 ounces equal a pound. Gather the produce you are purchasing, and estimate the weight of each item before weighing it. If you need one pound of grapes, ask your child to place the first bunch of grapes on the scale, and then estimate how many more or less grapes are needed to make exactly one pound. Let your child hold an item in each hand and guess which item weighs more. Then use the scale to check.

Ask questions to encourage thinking about measurement and estimation. You might want to ask your child:

➤ How much do you think six apples will weigh? More than a pound, less than a pound, or equal to a pound?

➤ How much do the apples really weigh? Do they weigh more or less than you estimated?

➤ Will six potatoes weigh more or less than the apples? How much do potatoes cost per pound? If they cost ten cents per pound, what is the total cost?

➤ Try weighing items using the metric system. How many grams does an apple weigh? How many kilograms does a sack of potatoes weigh? How does a kilogram compare to a pound?

Let your child experiment with the store scale by weighing different products.

Guess If You Can

Let your child think of a number between a stated range of numbers while you try to guess the number by asking questions. Here is a sample conversation.

Child: I am thinking of a number between 1 and 100.
Parent: Is it more than 50?
Child: No.
Parent: Is it an even number?

Child: No.
Parent: Is it more than 20 but less than 40?
Child: Yes.
Parent: Can you reach it by starting at zero and counting by 3's?
Child: Yes.
(At this stage, your child could be thinking of 21, 27, 33, or 39.)

After you have guessed your child's number, let your child guess a number from you by asking similar questions.

What Are the Coins?

What you will need: Some coins.

Ask your child the following questions:

➤ I have three coins in my pocket. They are worth 7 cents. What do I have? (a nickel and two pennies)
➤ I have three coins in my pocket. They are worth 16 cents. What do I have? (a dime, a nickel, a penny)
➤ I have three coins in my pocket. They are worth 11 cents. What do I have? (two nickels and one penny)
➤ I have three coins in my pockets. They are worth 30 cents. What do I have? (three dimes)
➤ I have six coins in my pocket. They are worth 30 cents. What could I have? (one quarter and five pennies or six nickels) This problem has more than one answer. It is challenging for children to experience problems like this.
➤ I have coins in my pocket, which have a value of 11 cents. How many coins could I have?

You get the idea! Give your child a few coins to figure out the answers.

Food Fun

When preparing a snack or meal, cut foods, such as a slice of bread, an apple or orange, into equal parts and talk about fractions with your child. If you have an 8-slice pizza, and there are four people in your family, how many slices of pizza are there for each person in your family?

Money Match—a game

1. The object of the game is to be the first player to earn a set amount (for example, 20 or 50 cents).
2. Each player rolls the dice and gets the number of pennies of the number shown on the dice.
3. As each player gets five pennies, a nickel replaces the pennies, and a dime replaces ten pennies or two nickels.
4. The first player to reach the set amount wins.

Test Preparedness

If your fourth grader is having difficulty with math facts, such as multiplication tables, create your own "pretests" at home. Follow a format similar to the test that your child's teacher uses. This will be a great drill for those pesky multiplication tables, and will calm some of those "test nerves."

SOCIAL STUDIES

FOURTH graders spend more time this year on social studies. They will explore government and community, as well as map reading and geography. Exposing your child to local history, many cultures and cultural events, as well as age-appropriate current event items bolster his ability in social studies.

Some General Tips

➤ Share family history with your children. Share your memories, and help your relatives and friends share family stories, too. Encourage your children to tell their own stories.
➤ Read historically based stories to your child. Was the story accurate? Was it fact or fiction?
➤ Watch television programs about topics related to the past with your children. Get library books on the same topics. Do the books and television programs agree?
➤ When you celebrate holidays explain to your child what is being celebrated and why. Help your child find stories or speeches about these holidays at the library or in a newspaper or magazine.

➤ Visit a local battlefield, historical home, or other significant landmark with your child.

➤ Get to know the history of the town or city where you live. Your newspaper may list parades, museum and art exhibits, children's theater, music events, and history talks and walks under "things to do." Choose some of these activities to do with your children.

➤ Attend festivals and fairs sponsored by a variety of ethnic, cultural, and community organizations.

➤ Make globes, maps, and encyclopedias available, and use every opportunity to refer to them. A reference to China in a child's favorite story, or the red, white, and green stripes on a box of spaghetti can be opportunities to learn more about the world.

Activities

Where Am I?

Find a map of your community. First find the approximate location of your house, then your street, and then find some familiar landmarks, such as the firehouse, grocery store, or school.

I Wish . . .

Make a wish list of places you would like to visit with your child. Look them up on a map. Create simple travel directions to that location.

Crossing the Line

While on a car trip, when crossing state lines, name the state capital, and other pertinent information about that state. These facts could include state flower, important cities, landmarks, and historical events. You can play a variation of this game by scouting for out-of-state license plates.

Teachers cannot do it all. They need our time, our support, and our consistent involvement.

—Washington Governor Gary Locke

SCIENCE

WATCH your little Einstein as she learns about the world around her. Your child will begin to recognize science as a major course of study this year. Encouraging her to learn more about science is easy because science IS the world around us. The air we breathe, the food we eat, the things we see—all are science lessons waiting to happen. It will be your mission to identify daily events as scientific experiments. While you will want to encourage a healthy interest in science and the world around your fourth grader, be sure to also stress safety. If your child is performing experiments or using a chemistry kit, you will want to be sure that your young child fully understands that bad things can happen to them. We don't want to scare our children away from science, but we must:

➤ Provide supervision when it is appropriate—for example, when using heat or mixing chemicals
➤ Teach children not to taste anything unless they know it is good for them and is sanitary
➤ Insist children wear goggles whenever fire or splatter could endanger eyes
➤ Teach children to follow warnings on manufacturers' labels and instructions
➤ Keep toxic substances, sharp tools, or other dangerous substances out of the reach of young children
➤ Teach children what they can do to minimize the risk of accidents
➤ Teach children what to do if an accident occurs

Below you will find many experiments and activities that you can enjoy with your fourth grader. Parents like yourself offered many of these tips, while others were recommended by the U.S. Department of Education.

General Tips

➤ Ask your children questions: How do you think the clock works? Why does a bird make a nest and what is the nest made of? How does the sun help us every day?

➤ Have your children make predictions about the weather or how fast a plant will grow or how high a piece of paper will fly with the wind. Have your children then test to see if their hunches are correct.

➤ Remind your child that it may take many tries before you get an answer. Keep trying.

➤ Have your children start collections of shells, rocks, or bugs, so that they can see similarities and patterns.

➤ Help your child recognize differences. He or she can look around the neighborhood to see the different animals and plants that live and grow there.

Activities

The Big Picture

Looking at objects closely is an important part of science, and a magnifying glass lets us see things we don't even know are there. It also helps us see how objects are similar or different from each other. Use your magnifying glass to see:

➤ What's hidden in soil or under leaves
➤ What's on both sides of leaves
➤ How mosquitoes bite
➤ Different patterns of snowflakes
➤ Butterfly wings
➤ How many different objects can you find in the soil?

Draw pictures, or describe what you see, in your notebook. If you were able to examine a mosquito, you probably saw how it bites something—with its proboscis, a long hollow tube that sticks out of its head. Snowflakes are fascinating because no two are alike. Powdery scales give butterfly wings their color.

GREAT IDEA!

Attack of the Straws

What you'll need: A raw potato, one or more straws.

Can a straw go through a raw potato? Here's an easy way to learn about inertia and momentum. Put a potato on the table or kitchen counter and hold it firmly with one hand, making sure the palm of your hand is not underneath the potato. With a fast, strong push, stab the potato with the straw. What happens? Did the straw bend? The straw should go into the potato. If it didn't, try again with another straw—maybe a little faster or harder.

An object remains at rest (the potato, in this case) or keeps moving (the straw, in this case) unless it is acted upon by some external force.

NOTE: IF THE POTATO IS OLD, SOAK IT IN WATER FOR ABOUT HALF AN HOUR BEFORE TRYING THIS ACTIVITY.

Slime!

What you'll need: 4 envelopes unflavored gelatin, square baking pan, a mixing bowl, liquid dish detergent, vegetable oil, 2 bowls, a watch with a second hand, a table knife, and an 8-ounce cup.

Oil the hinges of a door and it will stop squeaking. Rub petroleum jelly on lips to prevent them from becoming chapped. These slippery substances are called lubricants. They are very important in modern technology.

In a mixing bowl, dissolve the four envelopes of gelatin in two cups of hot tap water. Coat the inside of the pan with vegetable oil. Pour the gelatin mixture into the pan and put it in the refrigerator until firm (about three to four hours). Use the knife to cut the gelatin into cubes about 1 x 1 x 1 inch. You should have about 64 cubes. Place 15 cubes into a bowl. Place the second bowl about six inches (about 15 centimeters) away from the cube bowl. When your parent or a friend says "go," start picking up the gelatin cubes one at a time with your thumb and index finger (don't squeeze!). See how many cubes you can transfer to the other bowl in 15 seconds. Do not eat the gelatin cubes after they have been handled or after they are covered with lubricant. Put all the cubes back in the first bowl. Pour 1/4 cup dish detergent over the cubes. Gently mix the detergent and the cubes so that the cubes are well coated. Use the same method as before to transfer as many cubes as possible in 15 seconds. Throw away the cubes and detergent and wash and dry both bowls. Put about 15 new cubes into one bowl and pour 1/4 cup water over the cubes, again making sure the cubes are thoroughly coated. See how many cubes you can transfer in 15 seconds. Throw away the cubes and water. Put about 15 new cubes into one bowl. Pour 1/4 cup of vegetable oil over the cubes. Make sure they are well coated. See how many cubes you can transfer in 15 seconds. With which liquid were you able to transfer the most cubes? With which liquid were you able to transfer the fewest cubes? Which was the best lubricant (the slipperiest)? Which was the worst?

Cars, trucks, airplanes, and machines all have parts that rub against one another. These parts would heat up, wear down, and stop working if we didn't have lubricants. Lubricants reduce the amount of friction between two surfaces that move against each other.

Hair-Raising Results

What you'll need: A cool, dry day, 2 round balloons (inflated and tied), 2 20-inch pieces of string, 1 wool or acrylic sock, 1 mirror (or more), 1 friend (or more).

Have you ever been shocked when you walked across a rug or touched a light switch? Wait until a cool, dry day to learn about static electricity.

Tie a string to each inflated balloon. Rub a balloon on your hair for about 15 seconds. Be sure to rub around the whole balloon. What happens to your hair? What happens when you bring the balloon back close to your hair? Rub the balloon on your hair again and have a friend (or parent) do the same with the other balloon. Each of you holds the string to one balloon, letting the balloons hang freely, but without letting them touch anything. Slowly move the two balloons toward each other, but don't let them touch. What do you see? Do the balloons push away from each other, or do they pull toward each other? Place your hand between the two hanging balloons. What happens? Place a sock over one hand and rub one balloon with the sock. Then let the balloon hang freely. Bring your sock-covered hand near the balloon. What happens? Try rubbing both balloons with the sock and then let them hang near each other. What happens now? Look for other examples of static electricity around the house. Have you ever felt a shock when you touched a metal doorknob on a cold winter day? What often happens when you remove the clothes from the dryer?

All materials contain millions of tiny particles, called protons and electrons, that have electric charges. Protons have positive charges, and electrons negative ones. Usually, they balance each other, but sometimes when two surfaces rub together, some of the electrons rub off one surface onto the other and we can have static electricity. Materials with like charges (all positive or all negative) move away from each other; those with opposite charges attract each other.

Television

What you'll need: A television set, a VCR, if you have one.

Science can be learned from television. Even though the quality varies a lot, some programs provide a marvelous window on science.

Look on the regular networks, public television stations, and cable channels (The Discovery Channel, for example) for science programs such as *3-2-1 Contact, Nature, Nova, Newton's Apple, The Voyage of the MIMI, Mr. Wizard's World, National Geographic, Jacques Cousteau, Cosmos*, and *Smithsonian Institution* specials.

Look for reports of scientific discoveries and activities on regularly scheduled news programs, and for TV characters with science-related jobs—doctors, for instance. If you have a VCR, tape science shows so you can look at them later and stop—or replay—parts that are particularly interesting or hard to understand so you can explain them to your child.

Some TV programs give misleading information about science as well as about scientists. It is important to know which things on television are real and which ones aren't.

Scavenger Hunt

See if you can find . . .

- ➤ A simple machine
- ➤ A footprint made by an animal
- ➤ Something changed by the sun
- ➤ Something changed by the rain
- ➤ An animal that would fit inside a coffee cup
- ➤ One of the bodies of the Solar System
- ➤ Something that does not smell nice
- ➤ An example of pollution
- ➤ An insect

Recycle!

Take your child with you on your weekly trip to the recycling center. Learn where the objects you sorted are taken and what new products are made from it.

Become a Science Advocate

Visit your child's elementary school and see what kind of science instruction is available. During your visit, look for clues as to whether science is valued.

➤ Do you see displays related to science? Science learning centers?

➤ Are science-related drawings on the bulletin boards? Are there plants, terrariums, aquariums, or collections (of rocks or insects, for example)?

➤ Do you see any science equipment in evidence? Are there magnifiers? Magnets? Pictures? Films?

➤ Does the school library contain science books? If so, ask the librarian if the children are encouraged to read them.

➤ Is there enough space in the classrooms or elsewhere in the school for students to conduct experiments?

➤ In science classes, do students work with materials, or is the teacher always demonstrating?

➤ Do students discuss their ideas, predictions, and explanations with each other as well as with the teacher?

If you find the science program in your child's classroom to be inadequate, take action.

➤ If the science program is inadequate, talk with your child's teacher or meet with the principal. If that brings no results, write to or meet with school board members. You might get better results if you organize with other parents who have similar concerns.

➤ Volunteer your services to improve the science programs. You can:

■ Assist teachers and students with classroom science projects
■ Chaperone science-related field trips
■ Offer to set up a science display in the school's front hallway or in your child's classroom
■ Lead hands-on lessons (if you have a good science background yourself)
■ Help in a computer laboratory or other area requiring adult supervision
■ Volunteer to raise funds for computers, a classroom guinea pig, or field trips

FOREIGN LANGUAGE

FOREIGN language classes are becoming more common in our nation's elementary schools. Some elementary schools offer these classes for an hour or so each week, while other schools are adopting much more aggressive schedules for teaching/learning foreign languages. Foreign language offerings may vary depending on your geographical location. As we become part of a global community, there are more and more languages being offered to children of all ages. Children on the East Coast are likely to be offered classes in Italian or German. West Coast children often are given choices that also include Japanese or Chinese. Spanish and French, spoken by our neighboring countries, are commonly offered across the United States. There has also been a marked increase in hearing schools that offer American Sign Language as a foreign language option.

You can help your fourth grader better grasp foreign language skills, even if you do not speak the language he is learning. Remember that most fourth grade children will not be expected to be proficient in their foreign language studies, they will merely be becoming familiar with the language. They will be learning conversational words, and gaining a basic understanding of fundamentals of the language structure. While doing grocery shopping, housework, or gardening, ask your child to tell you the words for various items, using the foreign language he is studying.

Look for a book or recording of traditional folksongs in other languages. Chances are your child has sung "Frère Jacques" (Brother John) some time in her life. That may be a great starting point for getting her interested in French. The easy and fun melodies of folksongs make learning the words in another language easy. Try singing "Happy Birthday" in Spanish (Cumpleaños Feliz) or find a recording of children's songs in other languages to learn more.

GREAT IDEA!

MUSIC

CHILDREN typically enjoy music. They will sing, dance, and listen to music almost daily. Encouraging a healthy appreciation of all types of music while children are young creates a foundation of arts appreciation that can be carried along for a lifetime. Also, studies have shown that exposure and understanding of music can help a child in other subjects, such as math. Children in the fourth grade are often given the opportunity to rent or purchase musical instruments from the school or school-affiliated music store. Children are then offered weekly music lessons, specific to the chosen instrument, during school hours.

Some ways to encourage your musical fourth grader are:

➤ Provide your child with a wide array of music at home. Listen to all types of music—popular, classical, jazz, country, folk, and opera.
➤ Take your fourth grader to live musical performances. This could include choral concerts, religious events, or live performances.
➤ If possible, encourage instrumental lessons, such as piano.
➤ For a fun weekend, rent a video of a classic musical performance, such as *The King and I* or *My Fair Lady*.

Activities

Disc Jockey

Along with your child, sort your CD collection by musical type, or performer. Discuss the musician and the music with him while you sort. As a reward, allow him to choose CDs along the way to listen to, allowing him to associate the musical type with the artist.

LIBRARY

WHETHER at the local library, or the school media center, your fourth grader will enjoy exploring the world of books. Now that she is able to navigate through the shelves of information with ease, searching for a favorite author or genre of books, she will look forward to library visits with new zeal. This love of the written word should be nurtured. You can join her in her exploration of literature in many ways!

General Tips

➤ Include children in trips to the library, and go regularly.

➤ As soon as you can, help your child get a library card.

➤ Borrow recordings of children's stories and songs, cassette tapes, compact discs, videotapes, even puppets and educational toys.

➤ Find out if your library has computers and how your children can use them to learn or upgrade skills.

➤ Encourage your children to use the library to find information for their homework.

➤ Encourage your children to ask for help from you and the librarian in finding books and materials.

➤ Work with the librarian to teach older children how to find things in the library on their own.

➤ Teach your children how to take care of themselves in public places, especially if they use the library alone. Stress common sense guidelines for behavior in the library.

Activities

Play Librarian
Many children have a collection of books in their room. Have your child sort and organize his books, pretending he is the librarian.

ART

THERE are few people who do not have an interest in art. Some people's interests are more mature and sophisticated, while others enjoy a comfortable appreciation of painting, sculpting, sketching, or architecture. Children enjoy art in its most raw form from the time they are very young. Their eyes are drawn to certain colors and patterns—even while still in the crib. Now that your child is in fourth grade, she will be learning not only about shapes, colors, and art materials, but also about some famous artists and styles. You will want to have at least a few basic art materials and supplies around the house. No child should be without a box of crayons, markers, and colored pencils along with a modest supply of drawing and construction paper. These items are not only useful for art projects, but also for projects in other classes.

General Tips

➤ Let your child express himself. A picture doesn't have to look like something you can recognize.
➤ Have your child talk about the picture to describe what it is supposed to be. This also helps develop language skills.
➤ Encourage your child to make patterns of repeated colors and shapes. This helps develop an understanding of math as it relates to art.
➤ Have your child practice different techniques: create with soft lines, create with blocks of color, and create using different mediums.
➤ Have your child make connections between artwork and other subjects. Look at, and talk about, book illustrations when you are reading together.
➤ Check art books out of the library and look at famous paintings. Talk about what is in the picture and how the artist painted it. (Did he use thick paint with bold strokes or did she use light colors with dots of paint?)
➤ Display your child's art in your home and office.
➤ If your fourth grader is interested, enroll her in art classes.

PHYSICAL EDUCATION

TYPICALLY the fourth grade child is an active child. This level of activity eases your ability to encourage outdoor sports and games. Today's child will become sedentary if not encouraged to run, jump, bike ride, and play. Physical education is not only learning rules to a game, or exercising, but it involves learning to live a healthy lifestyle. Your child does not have to be the best athlete in the class, the fastest runner on the team, or the biggest kid on the court to be classified as "physically fit."

Some guidelines that you can use to build upon your child's awareness of physical education, health, safety, and fitness.

➤ Get involved in intramural sports programs at your school, YMCA, YWCA, or community center.

➤ Swimming lessons are often available at community centers or schools. Do sign your child up for these classes. It is not only a matter of fitness, but of safety as well.

➤ Provide opportunities at home to play and exercise

➤ Limit TV time to encourage other more physical activities.

➤ Encourage participation in team sports such as Little League baseball and American Youth Soccer Organization (AYSO) soccer.

➤ Encourage your child's interest in individual sports, such as tennis or golf.

➤ Encourage good hygiene.

➤ Be a good role model. Exercise regularly, take walks, and practice healthy habits.

Understand that not every child is going to be a star athlete, and that it's okay. There are many types of sports and athletics; you will certainly find one that suits both your child's physical abilities and personality. When considering athletics for your child, you may want to consider the following:

➤ What is my child interested in?

➤ Does she want to participate in one year-round sport or participate in several seasonal ones?

➤ Are the time, money, and emotional commitments realistic to my family's lifestyle?

➤ What is the coach's and league's philosophy? Do the coaches enjoy spending time with and working with athletes at my child's level?

➤ Do all of the children seem to be involved and having a good time?

➤ Do any members of my peer group have children who are also participating in this sport? If not, am I comfortable with the other parents whose children participate?

➤ Are both the equipment and location safe? What are the procedures should my child be injured?

Remember that athletics are just one part of physical education. Healthy children are also exposed to good nutritional and health habits.

COMPUTER

THE digital age has arrived, and it's here to stay. The presence of computers is evident in libraries, schools, and even in our homes. We have learned to use computers for entertainment, organizing, and productivity. Today's elementary school child often is more computer literate than his parents. Some of the reasons are the initiatives taken by some schools to provide advanced computer classes to children. Nowadays these advanced classes are commonplace and expected by the members of the parent community. Studies have shown that children who are given access to computers and computer literacy programs will often perform at a higher academic level than those who do not.

Affordable computer ownership programs abound! Look for bundled systems that include the computer, monitor, and printer. They can be found at your local department store, warehouse club, or online at websites like *www.dell.com* or *www.gateway.com*. Also, consider the iMac; it is affordable and easy to use.

While it is not mandatory that you own a computer, you may want to consider making the purchase. Both you and your child will benefit from the productivity tools and resources available with a computer. Many schools and teachers have websites where information such as homework assignments, lesson plans, lunch menus, and the school calendar is posted. Some teachers also post helpful resources and offer their e-mail address so that parents can easily contact them if necessary. If purchasing a home computer is not an option, make a concerted effort to schedule computer time at a local library or computer lab. If you are using a library or lab computer, help your fourth grader organize tasks before your allotted time so that his time is spent productively.

If you have a home computer, and are connected to the Internet, you will want to cover safety rules with your child. They need to know that they should:

➤ Never use the Internet without permission
➤ Never give out personal information such as their name, address, school, phone number, etc.
➤ Never give out your personal information
➤ Never give out passwords
➤ Only go to websites that have been given your stamp of approval
➤ Always ask you for help finding sites for a research project

SCHOOL SUPPLIES

PROVIDE educational materials at home. Be sure to include at least one educational gift on birthdays, Christmas, Hanukkah, Kwanzaa, or other special holiday. Some educational gifts would include: books, software, board games, workbooks, or art supplies.

You might also be asked to provide some or all of your child's classroom school supplies. There may be some items that will be provided by the school, but will require that you pay for them. Such examples could include subscriptions, teaching and learning aids, or admissions fees for field trips to local attractions. A sample list may include:

➤ 2 packages #2 pencils
➤ Crayons
➤ Colored pencils
➤ 2 glue sticks
➤ 1 bottle of glue
➤ 1 composition book
➤ Scissors
➤ Loose-leaf notebook paper
➤ Small school box
➤ 3 ring binder
➤ 2 packages 3 x 5 index cards
➤ 1 spiral notebook
➤ Section dividers with tabs
➤ school agenda/assignment book

SUMMARY

SUPPLEMENTING your child's education at home can be an enjoyable way to participate on your child's educational team. Eventually you will realize that supplementing your child's education is a natural way to spend quality time with your fourth grader. You will be providing your child with the skills and tools necessary to ensure his educational and social success.

4

Standardized Testing in School

TIMES certainly have changed. In the past, many parents were not even aware of their child's participation in standardized tests. The fact that a child was taking a standardized test was considered just as matter-of-factly as the fact that your child would be served a nutritious school lunch. Children got up, went to school, did schoolwork, and came home. Parents were not as involved, nor as influential in school policy, as the results–based parent of today. Today's parent is very aware of the term, "Standardized Test."

Merely the mention of standardized testing around a group of parents will likely receive a myriad of responses. Some will respond like one parent in my community, "I feel there should be a gentler way to monitor the success of our schools and the progress of our children." Others will accept them as a necessary tool to gauge the effectiveness of our school systems, and there will be others who are vehemently against such mass testing. Some parents believe that the tests shouldn't be made into an event. "Why worry the child?" they say. Those parents who reside in states where funding or student pro-motion is dependent on standardized test scores may be trembling either in anger or fear at the thought of these common tests. Parents in states where standardized testing is used solely as a baseline for performance and abilities may not have the same gut-wrenching reaction as the more test-centric states.

_____

CHANGING TIMES

When I was growing up, I don't think my mother had a clue as to when I was taking standardized tests. The exam would get passed out one day, and I would consider it a break from the teacher. Nobody ever explained the importance of not just filling in any oval when the test got too boring, or got into test-taking strategies. Now, in New York, my son takes exams most every year. We feed him big breakfasts, send him to bed early, and coach him on not just guessing and not answering if he doesn't know the correct choice. We are asked to do this by the school.

—A PARENT FROM NEW YORK

Regardless of where you fall in the debate spectrum, or reside geographically, standardized testing does seem to be a fixture in today's American education system. Fourth grade is one of the grades where standardized testing proves to be very important. It is possible that this is the first year that your child will be taking these tests; the tests that will translate to a better idea of how your fourth grader measures up to his peers, or perhaps more dollars for your school district. Understanding the role of testing will help you to enable your child to succeed in school and to develop a better relationship between your family and your child's school.

WHAT ARE STANDARDIZED TESTS?

TO understand the discussion surrounding standardized tests, parents must first understand what a standardized test is and how it is used. Standardized tests are created by commercial test publishers that analyze an array of specific state education standards in order to put together tests that cover a variety of material and wide range of abilities. Publishers of these tests engage the assistance of educators and specialists in this process, thus ensuring that they provide fair and reasonable measurement of the test-taking population. These tests are then administered to many students across the nation. Some widely accepted and commonly used tests throughout the country include the California Achievement Tests (CAT), the Stanford Achievement Test (SAT, but not to be confused with the college entrance exam), the Iowa Test of Basic Skills (ITBS), and the Stanford-Binet Intelligence Scale, to name a few. Texas and Pennsylvania are just two examples of states that have commissioned their own customized versions of standardized tests. Texas has the Texas Assessment of Academic Skills (TAAS) and Pennsylvania uses the Pennsylvania System of School Assessment (PSSA). Florida also uses a proprietary test, the Florida Comprehensive Assessment Test (FCAT).

Aptitude tests provide information about a person's future capabilities. Would your child make a good lawyer, craftsperson, or technician? **Achievement** tests provide metrics on the information already learned and understood by your child. Is your child proficient in math facts and reading comprehension?

There are two major types of standardized tests—aptitude and achievement. Aptitude type standardized tests give educators a view of student's innate abilities. These tests measure the child's ability to learn in the future, rather than what a child has already learned. Achievement tests, the tests most often referred to when discussing standardized tests, measure what a child has already learned, without regard to the child's growing ability to learn more in the future.

MEASUREMENT

STUDENTS are measured against other students of the same age and grade level. The collective results from standardized tests are used to measure a student's or school's performance. Student-focused results can give educators and parents a general idea of how a student is performing, where the student exhibits strong ability, and where a student may need extra help. Both aptitude and achievement tests are used to:

➤ Evaluate school programs
➤ Report on students' progress
➤ Diagnose students' strengths and weaknesses
➤ Select students for special programs
➤ Place students in special groups
➤ Certify student achievement (for example, award high school diplomas or promote students from grade to grade)
➤ Evaluate the overall performance of teachers

Standardized achievement tests usually focus on math and reading skills, while science and social studies may also be covered. Each of these areas is further broken down so that children's abilities can be assessed more granularly. In the math area of the test, children may be tested on basic computation skills, spatial relationships, and number relationships. In the reading module of the tests, children are commonly tested on reading comprehension, spelling, and vocabulary. Scores will be broken down and reported on accordingly, so that the entire educational team can have a basic idea of the exact strengths and weaknesses of a child, as shown in this one test.

Tests are given at different times of the school year, depending on the state you live in, and what test your child will be taking. Many states mandate that all standardized tests be given within small window of time after the first marking period, and usually after the holiday season has passed. This schedule allows teachers to prepare students for the test, and helps them identify possible weaknesses of the students. Because all fourth graders across a given state will be taking the test within the same window, the test results are easily comparable from school to school.

WHY IS MY CHILD BEING GIVEN THESE TESTS?

YOUR child's scores on these standardized tests help teachers and school administrators make important decisions about the effectiveness of the curriculum being taught. The scores obtained can help schools measure how students in a given class, school, or even the school system as a whole are performing against other students across the nation. The teachers, administrators, and involved parents can then help evaluate the meanings of these scores as they pertain to the school systems as a whole, a particular school within the school system, or even just one or two students.

A parent of fourth grade twins shares a wonderful example of the positive effect of standardized testing.

They tell the children that the school wants to know if the teachers are doing a good job and where the curriculum is weak. This is actually part of what they are looking for, since they changed the math curriculum a couple of years ago based on where the students were showing weaknesses.

—A PARENT FROM PENNSYLVANIA

Sometimes the standardized achievement tests are administered to students for reasons other than curriculum analysis. Sometimes teacher and school accountability questions are answered, although not always accurately, through the scores of these tests. Although these tests do provide a snapshot of the level of education students are receiving, it is important that all parties involved remember that there are many reasons why a child or group of children may not score well on the standardized tests. Children in low-income areas may score differently than children in affluent neighborhoods simply because of the quality of the school buildings, materials, or environmental stresses. They may score lower because of lack of materials, and lack of overall positive community morale. On the other side of the coin, they may score higher because teachers are forced to use extremely creative teaching methods to compensate for the lack of conventional teaching materials. For all of those reasons, test scores should reviewed using the proper level of perspective. Rather than looking at small details, administrators and parents may do themselves a favor by stepping back, charting trends, and reviewing the most drastic test variances.

Consider a school that has recently implemented a school breakfast program. They may use class work, quizzes, and standardized tests to note that children in the school district are more mentally sharp and active than they were before the implementation of the program. Another school district may use those trend statistics to confirm that providing parent outreach and involvement programs such as workshops and town meetings has facilitated a more supportive and successful school environment, funneling down to the children, who are better prepared to face their educational challenges. If you do not fully understand your school's reasons behind testing, and how those methods of reasoning affect your child, do not be shy about asking questions. Before the test ask:

➤ Which tests will be administered during the school year and for what purposes?
➤ How will the teacher or the school use the results of the tests?
➤ What other means of evaluation will the teacher or the school use to measure your child's performance?
➤ Should your child practice taking tests?

Answers will differ simply because there are various tests used across the United States, various reasons for testing, and a multiplicity of goals that educators and administrators wish to attain. Your school may test children to assess curriculum, evaluate teacher performance, or to gain funding. So, when you ask the questions, expect a myriad of answers, depending on the goals of your school, and the laws of your state. Do rest assured knowing that your child's test scores will not be shared with other parents.

After your child has taken the standardized test, you may have some questions. You may wonder how your fourth grader's performance on the standardized test affects other areas of his educational experience. To be completely informed, there are a few questions you should ask after the test:

➤ How do students in your child's school compare with students in other school systems across the country?
➤ What do the test results mean about your child's skills and abilities?
➤ Are the test results consistent with your child's performance in the classroom?
➤ Are any changes anticipated in your child's educational program?
➤ Are there things that you can do at home to help your child strengthen particular skills?

Teachers and administrators will usually take the time to be sure that you understand your child's test results, often sending home a paper explaining the computer readout that is your child's test result. You will undoubtedly be assured that the test is just one small gauge of your child's educational skills and abilities. When assessing your child, consider the whole child, her social skills, class work, range of interests, and emotional maturity. Unless your child's test scores show that she is especially weak, or especially strong in a discipline or disciplines, you will probably not see a change in her educational program, but your teacher may have suggestions that could bolster the scores on subsequent standardized tests.

While it is important to take these tests seriously, it is equally important that parents remember that these tests merely give teachers a window on a student's strengths and weaknesses. Ideally, teachers combine these test scores with other criteria to display an accurate view of a student's capabilities. These other criteria include:

➤ Observation of students in the classroom
➤ Evaluation of their day-to-day class work
➤ Grades on their homework assignments
➤ Meetings with their parents
➤ Close tracking of how students change or grow throughout the year.

Test scores for the same child can vary from day to day, depending on diet, sleep, and emotional preparedness. Parents can properly prepare a child for the test—getting the child to bed early, feeding the child a healthy balanced breakfast—and the child may still not perform up to level on a test. Remember that there are other factors that affect test taking. The child may not have received clear instruction on how to take the test, may not have followed instructions correctly, may have doubted the seriousness of the test, or simply felt uncomfortable in the test environment. For this reason, it is imperative to mention that these tests do indeed have limitations, inasmuch as their use in accurately gauging a child's academic ability as a stand-alone metric. If you are concerned about your school's use of standardized test results to track your child, you should talk with the teachers or administrators involved in order to obtain all the facts for your district.

Teachers should teach and forget the test. The test is used to measure reading comprehension and math skills. If the teaching methods work— there is no need to over-prepare students. Teachers should have confidence in their teaching ability and should have confidence in the kids!

—A PARENT FROM COLORADO

DO TEACHERS "TEACH THE TEST"?

TODAY'S parents and concerned citizens demand more accountability among educators than ever before. This heightened level of accountability has led to more emphasis being placed on standardized test scores. Parent–Teacher organizations, school administrators, and school board members will look to these scores to see if the educational needs of the student body are being met. It is hard to miss the sense of pride exuded from parents, administrators, and educators in schools that attain exemplary test scores.

The high level of emotion that accompanies the release of the test results leads to increased pressure among teachers to serve a platter of high test scores to the parents and administrators within their school system. Since the advent of standardized testing, teachers have "taught the test" on a minimal level. Teachers may have administered regular curriculum–based tests in a format similar to the standardized test result, even requiring children to fill in small ovals so that the child becomes familiar with the standard test answer sheet. Other teachers may have given timed tests, encouraging children to manage the time spent on each question. Teachers are also teaching according to the will of their supervisors. If a teacher is given a directive stating that the school system would like to see higher test scores in math, for instance, the teacher may focus on specific math skills, without mentioning that these particular skills would be those tested in standardized tests.

Of course, through the years, there have been claims of teachers spending time "teaching the test," rather than preparing our children for the future. While it is true that teachers may tailor some of their classroom instruction to better prepare their students for upcoming testing, parents will find that most teachers do not structure their entire day around test preparedness. Some parents

**TEN THINGS YOU CAN DO
TO HELP YOUR CHILD SUCCEED ON
A STANDARDIZED TEST**

1. What test? When?

    Bring up the issue early in the school year, perhaps even in your first conversation with your child's new teacher. Find out which tests your child will be taking this year and when.

2. Where are the weak spots?

    You need to determine, as honestly and intelligently as possible, the skills your child needs to improve most. The one person you should speak to is your child's teacher. Ask the teacher for specific suggestions on how your child might best prepare for the upcoming test. Most teachers will be happy to accommodate.

3. Review the rules and regulations

    You can diminish the tension of a "pencils down" test experience by explaining to your child why the test environment may be so demanding and her teacher may be so strict about adhering to the rules. Explain that standardized tests are reliable only to the extent that the same procedures are followed precisely everywhere.

4. Build confidence

    A lack of self-confidence is a serious issue with a significant portion of young children. You want your child to walk into that test room feeling good about himself and his abilities . . . so help him feel that way.

(continued)

consider themselves fortunate to have a teacher who is familiar with the test contents, and may therefore create classroom instruction to parallel the standardized achievement test given to fourth graders. Where the pressure of performing well on standardized tests is highest, students may be given sample practice tests that closely resemble the actual test.

HOW DO I PREPARE?

PARENTS, teachers, and students must all gear up for test day. As a parent, you may believe that the responsibility to prepare your child for the test falls upon your school. You are only partially correct. Parents need to take a realistic and calm look at standardized tests and the amount of preparation that their child may need to ensure the best possible test day. There are many skills that need to be mastered by your fourth grader by test day. Not only will she be expected to provide the correct answers to a wide variety of questions, she will be expected to sit quietly for an extended period of time, filling in small boxes or ovals with a #2 pencil. Time management will also be key. She will have a limited period of time to correctly answer as many questions as possible. So, you see, there are a lot of skills that you can help her sharpen. Columbia University Teachers College education expert Dr. Peter Cookson provides a comprehensive look at test preparedness tips and exercises in *A Parent's Guide to Standardized Tests*.

You may be coached by your school to help "prepare" your fourth grader to take a test successfully. Often a note is sent home letting you know when the test will be given, as well as some helpful tips—such as ensuring that your child has a good breakfast on test day, that she is dressed in comfortable clothes, or gets enough sleep the night before.

Remember that a child may become unnecessarily nervous about taking a test if he feels under undue pressure. Be sure to stress the importance of the test, without dwelling on it. Children have been reduced to tears after being unduly and unreasonably over-prepared for the test. The test looms over all of their daily activities. When test day comes, the child is a bundle of nervous energy, unable to clearly concentrate on the test booklet in front of him.

The U.S. Department of Education suggests that parents encourage and teach children good test-taking skills year-round—even when achievement tests are not imminent. Your calm approach to test taking has a calming effect on your child. Simple time management tasks, double-checking homework, and attention to detailed instructions can prove to be invaluable assets to your fourth grader. Some tips for positively impacting your fourth grader's test day include:

5. Don't create unrealistic expectations
This is the flip side of the previous suggestion. Fostering unreachable goals is as bad as squelching achievable goals. You want to impart to your child a balanced view of his prospects.

6. This is but one test
Make sure that your child understands this is only a single test, not a final judgment of her abilities. You can't fake this message. Your child will take the test results in proper perspective only if you do—and you should, because in fact, this really is just one test.

7. Set up a study schedule
Establish a reasonable time (not the end of the day when children are tired) and find a comfortable, quiet place to study. Make sure everyone else in the family understands that during study time your child is not to be disturbed.

8. Take care of the test accessories
Make sure your child is prepared for the test the night before. Collect the necessary accessories such as #2 pencils, an eraser, and a calculator (if allowed). A good night's sleep is important, as is a proper breakfast the morning of the test. Do these things to minimize stress and anxiety that day.

9. Keep cool
It can't be said enough: Relax. Frantic parents will only make their child even more nervous than necessary. Keep your calm and that will set an example for your child.

10. Try to have fun
You really don't need to dread standardized tests; they don't have to be painful experiences.

➤ Meet with your child's teacher as often as possible to discuss progress. Ask the teacher to suggest activities for you and your child to do at home to help prepare for tests and improve your child's understanding of schoolwork. Parents and teachers should work together to benefit students.

➤ Make sure your child attends school regularly. Remember, tests do reflect children's overall achievement. The more effort and energy a child puts into learning, the more likely your child will do well on tests.

➤ Provide a quiet, comfortable place for studying at home.

➤ Make sure that your child is well rested on school days and especially the day of a test. Children who are tired are less able to pay attention in class or to handle the demands of a test.

➤ Give your child a well-rounded diet. A healthy body leads to a healthy, active mind. Most schools provide free breakfast and lunch for economically disadvantaged students. If you believe your child qualifies, talk to the school principal.

➤ Provide books and magazines for your youngster to read at home. By reading new materials, a child will learn new words that might appear on a test. Ask your child's school about a suggested outside reading list or get suggestions from the public library.

SUMMARY

ALTHOUGH many parents and educators have differing views on the benefits of these types of tests, it seems as though standardized testing is going to be commonplace in our education systems for many years to come. Until a methodology is found to evaluate all students, teachers, and schools equally, these tests may provide the best measurement of our children, our educators, and our school districts. In fact, standardized testing may possibly be the best method to measure our nation's educational preparedness as a whole.

Those facts aside, test time can be extremely stressful for all involved. Most teachers do not enjoy the pressure of teaching the test any more than parents or students like the burden of feeling as though test performance is the end all and be all of a child's education. Adequate test preparation and performance, as well as evaluation of the child's total educational skills should still remain paramount in everyone's mind. Test scores should be considered only a portion of a child's total measure of educational ability and success. Understand the test, prepare the child, discuss any concerns with the other members of your educational team, and most of all remember that these tests do not measure the all-important qualities of citizenship, good values, and wholesome personality.

Standardized testing is always changing. At the time of publication, the information listed below was accurate. It is important to contact your child's school early in the year to confirm what tests are going to be given, what topics will be covered, and when the tests will be given.

States that require standardized testing in fourth grade include:

ALABAMA

Name of test:	SAT 9
Subjects covered:	Reading, Writing, Math, Science, Social Science
Month given:	April

ARIZONA

Name of test:	SAT 9
Subjects covered:	Reading, Writing, Math
Month given:	March

ARKANSAS

Name of test:	SAT 9
Subjects covered:	Reading, Writing, Math
Month given:	April

CALIFORNIA

Name of test:	SAT 9 and Standardized Testing and Reporting (STAR)
Subjects covered:	Reading, Writing, Math
Month given:	March

COLORADO

Name of test:	Colorado Student Assessment Program (CSAP)
Subjects covered:	Reading, Writing
Month given:	March/April

CONNECTICUT

Name of test:	Connecticut Mastery Test (CMT)
Subjects covered:	Reading, Writing, Math
Month given:	September/October

DELAWARE

Name of test: Delaware Student Testing Program (DSTP)

Subjects covered: Science, Social Science

Month given: N/A

FLORIDA

Name of test: Florida Comprehensive Assessment Test (FCAT)

Subjects covered: Reading

Month given: January/March

IDAHO

Name of test: Iowa Test of Basic Skills (ITBS)

Subjects covered: Reading, Writing, Math

Month given: October/November

ILLINOIS

Name of test: Illinois Standards Achievement Test (ISAT)

Subjects covered: Science, Social Science, Health, Fine Arts

Month given: April

IOWA

Name of test: Iowa Test of Basic Skills (ITBS)

Subjects covered: Reading, Writing, Math

Month given: N/A

KANSAS

Name of test: Criterion Based State Assessment

Subjects covered: Math, Science

Month given: February/March

KENTUCKY

Name of test: Commonwealth Accountability Testing System (CATS)

Subjects covered: Reading, Writing, Math

Month given: April/May

LOUISIANA

Name of test: Criterion-Referenced Test (CRT)

Subjects covered: Language Arts, Science, Social Studies, Math

Month given: March

MAINE

Name of test:	Maine Educational Assessment (MEA)
Subjects covered:	Reading/Writing, Math, Science, Social Science, Arts
Month given:	March/November/December

MASSACHUSETTS

Name of test:	Massachusetts Comprehensive Assessment System (MCAS)
Subjects covered:	Reading, Writing, Math
Month given:	April/May

MICHIGAN

Name of test:	Michigan Educational Assessment Program (MEAP)
Subjects covered:	Reading, Math
Month given:	May

MISSISSIPPI

Name of test:	Terra Nova
Subjects covered:	Reading, Writing, Math
Month given:	May

MISSOURI

Name of test:	Missouri Assessment Program (MAP)
Subjects covered:	Math, Social Studies
Month given:	April/May

MONTANA

Name of test:	Iowa Test of Basic Skills
Subjects covered:	Reading, Writing, Math, Science, Social Science
Month given:	March

NEVADA

Name of test:	Terra Nova
Subjects covered:	Reading, Writing, Math, Science, Social Science
Month given:	October

NEW JERSEY

Name of test:	Elementary School Proficiency Assessment (ESPA)
Subjects covered:	Language Arts, Math, Science
Month given:	May

NEW MEXICO

Name of test:	Mew Mexico Achievement Assessment
Subjects covered:	Writing, Math
Month given:	March

NEW YORK

Name of test:	Fourth Grade Assessment
Subjects covered:	Reading, Math
Month given:	January/May

NORTH CAROLINA

Name of test:	North Carolina Testing Program End of Grade Test (EOG)
Subjects covered:	Reading, Writing, Math
Month given:	last month of school

NORTH DAKOTA

Name of test:	Terra Nova
Subjects covered:	Reading, Writing, Math, Science, Social Science
Month given:	March

OHIO

Name of test:	Ohio Proficiency Test
Subjects covered:	Reading, Writing, Math, Citizenship, Science
Month given:	March

OKLAHOMA

Name of test:	Norm Referenced Test (NRT)
Subjects covered:	Reading, Language Arts, Math
Month given:	N/A (currently contingent on funding)

RHODE ISLAND

Name of test:	National Assessment of Educational Progress (NAEP), New Standards English Language Arts Reference Exam, New Standards Mathematics Reference Exam
Subjects covered:	Reading, Writing, Math
Month given:	February/March

SOUTH CAROLINA

Name of test: Palmetto Achievement Challenge Test (PACT)
Subjects covered: Reading, Writing, Math
Month given: April/May

SOUTH DAKOTA

Name of test: SAT 9
Subjects covered: Reading, Writing, Math, Science, Social Science
Month given: March/April

TENNESSEE

Name of test: Tennessee Comprehensive Assessment Program
                       (TCAP)
Subjects covered: Reading, Writing, Language Arts, Math, Science,
                       Social Science, Spelling
Month given: March/April

TEXAS

Name of test: Texas Assessment of Academic Skills (TAAS)
Subjects covered: Reading, Writing, Math
Month given: May

UTAH

Name of test: Criterion-Referenced Test (CRT)
Subjects covered: Reading/Language Arts, Math, Science
Month given: March/April

VERMONT

Name of test: Vermont Comprehensive Assessment System
                       (VCAS)
Subjects covered: Language Arts, Math
Month given: March

VIRGINIA

Name of test: SAT 9
Subjects covered: Reading, Writing, Math
Month given: April or May (school's choice)

WASHINGTON

Name of test: Criterion-Referenced Test (CRT)

Subjects covered: Reading, Writing, Math
Month given: April/May

WASHINGTON, DC
Name of test: SAT 9
Subjects covered: Reading, Writing, Math
Month given: April

WEST VIRGINIA
Name of test: SAT 9
Subjects covered: Reading, Writing, Math, Science, Social Science
Month given: April

WISCONSIN
Name of test: Wisconsin Knowledge and Concepts Examination (WKCE)
Subjects covered: Reading, Writing, Math, Science, Social Studies
Month given: February/March

WYOMING
Name of test: Wyoming Comprehensive Assessment System (WyCAS)
Subjects covered: Language Arts, Math
Month given: April

SAMPLE READING QUESTIONS

READING tests consist of a few different reading passages generally about one page in length. These passages are followed by multiple-choice questions that cover vocabulary, main ideas, and details about the story.

"What do you mean, there's nothing to do?" Grandmother asked gently. She noticed that Elena looked a little down.

"Well, I finished my book, and now I don't have anything to do." Elena's normally cheerful face looked <u>gloomy</u>.

   1. In this story, Elena feels gloomy. <u>Gloomy</u> means
     a. puzzled.

b. hopeful.

c. excited.

d. unhappy.

Before I go on with this story, I should also tell you that I practically worshipped my brother Kris. Kris was so cool. After all, he was a teenager, and anything he did, I wanted to do. If Kris was riding his bike, I wanted to ride my bike. If Kris was jumping off a bridge, I wanted to jump off a bridge. If Kris was going to breathe oxygen in and carbon dioxide out, I wanted to . . . well, you get the picture.

2. The second paragraph is mostly about how the boy
   a. wanted to go to the barber.
   b. felt about his older brother.
   c. spent his summer vacation.
   d. worried about being left out.

Many modern mountain bikes have <u>suspension systems</u> that take out a lot of the bumps and jolts. This gives the rider a much smoother ride. The brakes have also been improved so that riders can slow down and stop more safely. All in all, these changes make mountain bikes much easier to ride.

3. In this passage, the words <u>suspension systems</u> means the same as
   a. springs that let the wheels move up and down over bumps.
   b. brakes that allow a bike rider to stop more safely.
   c. hooks for hanging your mountain bike on the wall.
   d. balloon-like tires that grip the road.

SAMPLE MATH QUESTIONS

1. Which value is **NOT** the same as the others?
   a. 1.14
   b. 1.25
   c. $\frac{5}{4}$
   d. $1\frac{1}{4}$

2. Study this number pattern.

7, 10, 13, 16, __, 22, 25

What is the missing number?

a. 17

b. 18

c. 19

d. 20

3. Miss Duval ordered 420 bath towels to sell in her store. The towels were packed in 12 boxes when they arrived. If each box had the same number of towels, how many towels were in each box?

a. 33

b. 35

c. 41

d. 350

5

Your Child's Social Development

WITH all of this discussion about the fourth grade academic "transition year," you may be hoping for a calm and serene year of emotional and social growth, right? Be forewarned that the term "transition year" does not just apply to the academic life of a fourth grader, but to the social skills and development, as well. This year's child is in such a state of transition that parents are often left unbalanced; unsure what to expect. Your son or daughter may be pleasant and agreeable one minute, sharp and upset the next. The fourth grade child thinks independently, yet prefers to be part of a group. Because the fourth grade student is acutely aware of his classmates, he may measure himself against an unrealistic set of metrics, often leading to a low level of self-esteem. He may be so aware of how others are doing in the class, who is intelligent, who is pretty, who is athletic, that he rarely sees himself as one of the cream of the crop. This energetic child may sometimes be plagued with poor appetite and difficulty sleeping. Some typical traits of a fourth grader are:

- ➤ Acceptance of responsibility
- ➤ Extremely energetic
- ➤ Works responsibly and independently
- ➤ Begins to plan and organize
- ➤ Poor appetite, inconsistent sleep patterns
- ➤ Lanky, slouched posture
- ➤ Concerned about the world around him, not fantasy
- ➤ Understands the word "trust" and appreciates it
- ➤ Aims to please
- ➤ Boys may be increasingly less concerned about their physical appearance, while girls may be meticulous about their appearance
- ➤ Dresses according to peer group
- ➤ May set unrealistic standards and will be upset when not met
- ➤ Has mood swings, cries easily
- ➤ Begins hero worship of older members of the same sex
- ➤ May have physical habits such as: fingers in hair, picking at nails, nail biting
- ➤ Differentiates and assigns importance to right and wrong, and being fair

Your son or daughter is teetering on the cusp between childhood and teenhood. These "tween" years can be difficult for parents and children alike. It is no wonder that parents of fourth graders sometimes look ahead to the teen years with extreme dismay. Occasionally, your fourth grader can be observed playing with toys and games suited for younger children, and you will smile inside, reminiscing of the days when he willingly climbed on your lap, or invited you to play with him. You may still experience moments of closeness, and occasionally you will witness moments when your fourth grader plays with his more "babyish" toys, but those moments will probably be fleeting, at best.

Your fourth grader struggles internally to understand the mixed feelings churning within her. Her strong sense of truthfulness and right may conflict with her yearning to please those in her peer group. She agonizes over the decision to be true to herself rather than to her friends. And, on top of everything else, your fourth grader may be experiencing some of the early symptoms of puberty. Providing a healthy fourth grade classroom atmosphere and supportive home environment can affect the success of a fourth grader as she constructively trudges through her mixed feelings about the more grown up self she is becoming.

PEER INTERACTIONS

CHILDREN in the fourth grade are pack creatures. Where you find one fourth grader, you will often find many. You may remember a time when your child spent large stretches of time with you, enjoying your company. As your child got older, he learned to spend time alone; playing, reading, and daydreaming. While the fourth grader will still enjoy one-on-one time with a parent or loved one, and will frequently be found working and playing independently, he exceedingly loves to spend time with his friends and classmates. But take heart, this group dynamic is a positive phenomenon. Basic lessons in cooperation, citizenship, and responsibility are learned in these group situations. Some of the best opportunities for your child to spend time with his peer group outside of the classroom are through special groups and clubs, such as sports or scouting.

Interest or Peer Group?

Don't be surprised when your child bounds home from school one day, plops a heavy backpack onto the floor and expresses an interest in a new club or activity. Instead, take note that you are being made aware of some of the interests incubating within your child's soul. You might not have realized that your fourth grader wanted to become involved in music, for instance, until she came home and announced that she is joining the elementary school choir. Equally surprising will be her request, a mere two weeks later, asking for karate lessons.

Understand that your fourth grader is being driven by two distinct powers: interest and peer group. An activity or item must contain a perceived value in one of those categories in order to be considered by a fourth grader. Their subconscious will assign value to an item or activity by asking, "Am I interested in this? Are my friends and classmates interested in this?" Whenever your fourth grader comes to you with new requests, invitations to events, or even with a gift idea list, remember those phrases—interest and peer groups. Consider if your fourth grader really wants something, or if he is reacting to what the peer group is transmitting as the something that your fourth grader should want. There is a difference. Does your fourth grader want this item because he has an interest in it, or does he want it because he feels that his friends want him to have an interest in it. Sometimes you may give in, even when the request seems to be dictated by the peer group, and allow your child something that you may believe to be frivolous, as long as the financial, emotional, or time commitments do not outweigh the benefits received by your child. On other occasions, where the commitments outweigh any benefits your fourth grader will receive, you will probably want to exercise patience. If, after an appropriate waiting period, your fourth grader is still asking for something, you might want to reconsider; has he taken on a new interest? Alternatively, you can use these situations to your child's benefit by having discussions about individuality, being a leader rather than a follower, and the advantageous of being able to say "no." Use these small vignettes to teach your child how to ignore peer group pressure, because he will certainly need the strength as he gets older.

Belonging to a group is very important to your fourth grader, and she may have decided to join elementary choir simply to be with friends; this is an illustration of an activity being driven by the peer group. When she asked herself, "Are my friends and classmates interested in this?" she found that the activity was valued by her peers, and therefore she should value this activity as well. Peer group decisions are also responsible for many of the fad items that children ask for on their gift idea lists or while doing school shopping. Children who make decisions driven by their peer group will be aware of their classmates and friends, and the unspoken rules of being included in the group.

Another fourth grader who decides to join the elementary choir may love music, and find that singing brings him a lot of pleasure; this is an illustration of an activity being driven by interest. Although none of his friends value involvement in the elementary choir, his subconscious answered affirmatively when asked, "Am I interested in this?" Although there may be few friends and peers involved in the activity chosen by this fourth grader, he will immensely enjoy the decision he made independently.

Peer Pressure

As illustrated above, your child is becoming more aware of her place in her peer group than ever before. It is important to her that she is considered an important member of the group, and that she is accepted. As mentioned earlier in this chapter, the fourth grader is a pack creature, always aware of the other members of the group, and their activities. This can be wonderful for you and your fourth grader, or extremely problematic.

If other children who share the same goals and morals that you have instilled in your child surround your child, the group will bring out the best in each member. The children of the group will police each other, so to speak. Breaking the unspoken and unwritten code of morals that the group has adopted will usually be met with scorn by the other members of the group. This sort of self-policing is advantageous to the entire group, and your child benefits from being involved in this group of children. It is not uncommon for one of the group to stray from the unspoken group morals, perhaps by taunting or teasing another child. When this happens, the other peer group members are not shy about expressing their disapproval. The resulting peer tribunal may seem harsh, and sometimes is very distressing to the dissenting peer member, but serves as a method of self-policing. Knowing that the others in the group will frown upon straying from the moral guidelines commonly followed by the whole will serve as a positive, guiding each member of the group away from the new temptations.

There is also the possibility that your child is a member of a peer group comprised of children who do not share the same morals or ideals that you have attempted to instill in your child. If your child is involved in a group like this, you may notice some changes in behavior. A typically respectful child may become antagonistic or difficult. If the other children in the group do not excel academically, you may notice a slip in your child's grades or homework efforts. Unfortunately, this example of the peer group dynamics does not serve as a positive to your fourth grader. In this year of exposure to new temptations, your child needs to be guided by a positive moral compass. If your child surrounds himself with a value defunct group of children, he may morally dumb down to better fit in with the group. The opinions of the group will weigh heavily on him. When the rest of the group teases or picks on a weaker child, he may join in, just to be part of the group. He will not want to be perceived as weak or soft to the rest of the group. Breaking free from this situation can be difficult for your fourth grader, and he will need a lot of support and guidance from you. Be ready to help your fourth grader make the transition to a new peer group. Offer alternative activities and friends to him; having access to a new peer group will provide the strength to break free of the negative influences.

Parents of fourth grade children commonly relate stories about their well-behaved children suddenly becoming more difficult, mouthy, or perhaps even using foul language. It's likely that this could be attributed to your child's peer group—especially the foul language. Children of this age are mirrors of the other children with which they interact, and using "swear words" is often confused with fitting in or being cool. Let your child know that this is unacceptable behavior, and encourage him to hold onto the language rules at home and at school.

Friendships

Gently guiding your child toward making good friendship decisions could help you avoid some behavior difficulties. Undoubtedly your fourth grader will make friends with children that you do not know. You will want your child to be armed with the tools necessary to make good friendship decisions. It is always a good idea to attempt to get to know your child's friends, and their parents, if possible. The more you know about your fourth grader's interactions and relationships, the better equipped you are to help when there are times of trouble.

When you meet your child's friends, observe the interaction between the two. You will immediately gain important clues to the friendship. Which of the two is the dominant? Which is the follower? How likely is your child to be influenced by this new friend, and is that a positive or negative? Chances are that you will be exceedingly happy with the friendship choice your child has made, but there are exceptions.

Sometimes our children make poor friendship decisions. They may choose a friend that just does not seem to be a healthy match for them. Your quiet, sensitive daughter may now be friends with a group of conniving girls—girls she has avoided in past years. She becomes a subservient member of their group, allowing herself to be bossed around and manipulated. To extract herself from this situation, or at least gain the respect of these girls, she may herself become manipulative and conniving, trying to beat the others at their own game. Remember that our children make decisions based on two things, interest and peer group. It is very possible that your child has decided to befriend someone simply because the other children in the class have befriended this child. Do not berate your child for choosing this friend, but talk with her later, in private, and provide her with tools and insights. When you discuss this friendship with your child, she may begin to see for herself that it is a friendship she does not plan on nurturing. It is important that you let your child come to this decision, and that you do not make it for her. Don't forget; the lessons your child learns this year about friendships are extremely important.

Conflicts

Children of this age thrive in group activities, no matter what the driving force is behind their participation. They thoroughly enjoy being in the company of friends and classmates. In school, on playgrounds, and around the neighborhood, groups of children will naturally gravitate to each other, laughing, joking, and playing with an unrestrained exuberance. Boys will tend to play with other boys, and girls will gather with other girls. Sometimes they will play together, but often they will engage in a battle of the sexes mentality, challenging each other to contests and games.

Unfortunately, this constant, highly energetic interaction lends itself well to conflicts and bumps in the friendship road. The voracity with which the fourth grade child plays, as well as the pack atmosphere shared by these children creates a volatile environment. A silly prank may become a huge fracas, children yelling and crying, viciously protecting, or sometimes attacking, their friend and comrade. The most common weapons used in these battles are simply words; sharp, painful words. Parents and teachers are witnesses to the aftermath of the battles. They hear the stories, as passed on from the nine-year-olds that participated. "Joey said that he doesn't like me anymore because I'm not good at soccer!" or "Amy won't be my friend anymore because I am friends with Tina."

The fourth grade battles, while often very heated, usually do not have long-lasting effects. The children use some of their newfound reasoning and bargaining skills to come to a compromise, and before you know it, Joey is not so angry about the failed block, and Amy doesn't mind that your fourth grader is also friends with Tina. While each of these battles may be difficult and emotionally draining for both you and your child, understand that with each of these fights, your fourth grader is gaining skills. These skills include the ability to compromise, resolve conflict, and get along with others.

First Crushes

Imagine how confused your fourth grader was on the day that he woke up and realized that girls did not have cooties, or when she found out that boys were not gross. For years those were the truths in life: girls have cooties, boys are gross. It was easy enough; the rules were simple. The two genders endured each other at school, worked together, but never saw each other as anything different than cootie-bearing, gross creatures. Waking up to find that girls were sort of cool, or boys were sort of nice to be around, sent the children running for support.

For that reason, you will find that fourth grade boys are apt to congregate with other fourth grade boys, and that fourth grade girls will enjoy the company of other fourth grade girls. While in the familiar surroundings of their own gender, the children are able to ignore the pangs of their first childhood crushes. Wrapping themselves in the comfort of their same-gendered schoolmates and friends gives the child the ability to ignore the confusing feelings they are experiencing about the opposite gender. That aside, don't be surprised if your fourth grader comes home from school daydreaming about a certain classmate. This is the year where first crushes are often experienced, and are sometimes publicly proclaimed.

If your child comes home talking about a particular member of the opposite sex, family members or friends may be tempted to tease him about this newfound interest. Do your very best to squash the teasing remarks and comments. Your child already feels very vulnerable in the unfamiliar world of "crushes." Teasing now builds walls that affect the future. As your child gets older, and learns more about relationships, you will want him to feel comfortable coming to you for support. If you tease now, he might not share information with you in the future, for fear of being ridiculed or mocked. Do not allow yourself or others to humiliate or embarrass your fourth grader while he or she is experiencing this new emotional sensation.

> You may remember Judy Blume's *Tales of a 4th Grade Nothing* and *Are You There God? It's Me, Margaret* with great fondness. Perhaps you can introduce these titles to your child this year, as their perennial popularity proves that the topics covered ring true to fourth graders. Find these titles and other Judy Blume books in your local bookstore, or search Amazon.com.

THE ONSET OF PUBERTY

CHILDREN grow at different rates, as we all know. It may be hard to believe, but some children in the fourth grade are experiencing the early stages of puberty. The emotional and physical turmoil experienced can create a lot of stress for both parent and child, especially during this turbulent year of growth.

Be prepared to discuss some difficult topics with your child. If you have not already done so, open those lines of communication. We all shuffle our feet a little when it comes to discussing very adult topics with our children, so don't feel alone as you stumble over the correct terminology when discussing menstruation with your now pre-teen daughter or erections with your prepubescent son. There are some wonderful resources available to parents to help them explain the physical and emotional changes that take place during puberty. Find the resource that is right for you, choose the time that is right, but don't procrastinate. You are the best source of information your child has. If you do not supply him or her with the proper information about the changes incurred during puberty, who will?

Be especially sensitive to your son or daughter if they are beginning puberty before their friends. At this early age, puberty can be both a mystery and a curse. Being the first girl in the class to wear a bra is not always a proudly worn badge. Your daughter may feel uncomfortable in her differences, knowing that she is looked at differently now that her body is developing. She may suddenly become reserved, or less apt to participate in sports activities. Your son, although experiencing less obvious outward signs of puberty, may also be confused and embarrassed by the hormonal and physical changes his body is experiencing. He may be affected by mood swings that cause him to cry at the drop of a hat. Frank and maturity-appropriate discussion will be beneficial to the emotional well being of the child.

I went to a class with my son that was put together by school counselors—preparing us for puberty with our kids. It was wonderful. I got to know my son a little better and vice-versa. It was a special time for

the two of us. It helped talking to other parents about the fears and challenges of puberty.

—A PARENT FROM IOWA

SELF-ESTEEM

SOCIAL growth cannot be discussed without mentioning self-esteem, the feelings that one has about oneself. The fourth grader's self-esteem is at a very delicate stage. The fourth grade student is typically unable to attain the high goals he set for himself; thereby sabotaging his self-esteem before it ever has the opportunity to blossom. They will constantly degrade and find fault with their work and the things that they do, they may be overly skeptical of themselves. This unease with their sense of self is further degraded by the emotional seesaw they are teetering on. Even those children who seem to be on top of the world may sometimes struggle with how they feel about themselves.

The increasing level of importance that a fourth grade child places on her peer group directly affects their self-esteem level. Because children place value on what their peer group thinks, they may believe that they are unable to live up to the values expected by the group. This further leads to a sense of low self worth. Increasingly the fourth grade child believes that without the group, she is unimportant. She may believe that she is not pretty enough, smart enough, cannot run fast enough, or is not rich enough to be valued by the group. For all of these reasons, it is important that the adults in a fourth grader's life are supportive and caring.

Children suffering from low self-esteem often believe that they are unimportant to the adults around them. This leads to the child feeling, often without good reason, insecure, unsafe, and unloved. Note your child's test scores, energy level, and behavior—all can be clues to a child suffering from low self-esteem.

Children with healthy self-esteem levels are able to set realistic goals and expectations for themselves. They do not measure themselves against the values of their peers, but against the values they feel comfortable with. These children are very comfortable in their relationships with the adults around them, and bask in feelings of security and safety. All of these combine to create a child who is well-adjusted and best equipped to face the many challenges of the preteen world.

Self-esteem is not acquired all at once nor do children always feel good about themselves in every situation. A child may feel self-confident and accepted at home but not around the neighborhood or in school. Furthermore, as children interact with their peers or learn to function in school or some other place, they may feel accepted and liked one moment and feel isolated and unsure the next. You can help by giving consistent and honest reassurance to your child. Your approval, appreciation, and admiration will balance the scales of self-esteem.

Want to give your child an interesting new challenge? Have your child sit down and write down everything he likes about himself. Also encourage him to write down the three qualities about himself that he thinks are most important. This exercise will allow him to focus on the positive.

The U.S. Department of Education reminds us about some important findings about self-esteem:

➤ The family is a strong force in the development of self-esteem. The early years are particularly important in establishing an "authentic and abiding self-esteem" in a person.

➤ High parental self-esteem is crucial to the ability to nurture high self-esteem and personal effectiveness in children.

➤ School climate plays an important role in the development of the self-esteem of students. Schools that target self-esteem as a major school goal appear to be "more successful academically as well as in developing healthy self-esteem among their students" according to the California Task Force to Promote Self-Esteem.

➤ Self-esteem and achievement may be either the cause or the effect of each other, depending upon the person and the particular situation in which they function.

➤ Young girls who possess positive self-esteem are less likely to become pregnant as teenagers.

➤ Persons who hold themselves in high esteem are less likely to engage in destructive and self-destructive behavior including child abuse, alcohol and drug abuse, violence and crime.

➤ Exclusive attention to just self-esteem or personal achievement may well result in less favorable outcomes in either or both areas than when an approach is used which attends to both self-esteem and achievement.

➤ The choice to esteem oneself or not is ultimately the responsibility of the individual no matter what the background and prior experiences of the individual may be. High self-esteem can never be given to a person by another person or society. It must be sought, "earned" by the individual for him or herself.

Nurturing your child's self-esteem should be an ever-present topic on your mind. Your fourth grader is increasingly aware of what his peer group thinks, and how he compares to their value system. It is up to you and the other members of your child's educational team to help build upon a child's self-esteem, equipping him with the tools necessary to become a participant in healthy relationships, and giving him the strength to dismiss those that can be detrimental or dangerous. Encourage your child by giving him honest and sincere praise when deserved. Children are very bright and will recognize if you are being patronizing or insincere in your kind words. This can cause more harm than good, leading the child to believe that you are lying just to make him feel good.

Clearly define your family's morals and values so that your child has a clear idea of what to strive for in life. Treat your child with respect, even when they are not showing you the respect that you deserve or expect. Show them the correct ways to deal with conflicts. Do not offend or degrade them, but show them the correct way to interact with others. You will be portraying a good role model to your child, showing them how to communicate with others, and disciplining if necessary, while allowing them to escape with their core level of self-esteem intact.

Interact with your child. Ask your fourth grader for her opinion, then listen while she gives it. You might not always agree with it, but allowing her to speak freely to you about her thoughts, in a respectful manner, will further bolster her self-esteem levels. Furthermore, provide feedback, sharing your opinions and thoughts, and encourage an open dialogue. Not only does this provide evidence of the esteem you have for your child, it also keeps those important doors of communication open so that you can discuss increasingly difficult topics as your child grows.

You can help your child develop and maintain healthy self-esteem by helping him cope with defeats, rather than emphasizing constant successes and triumphs. During times of disappointment or crisis, your child's weakened self-esteem can be strengthened when you let the child know that your love and support remain unchanged. When the problem has passed, you can help your child reflect on what went wrong. The next time this occurs, your child can use the knowledge gained from overcoming past difficulties to help cope with a new crisis. Also, do not be afraid to admit your own shortcomings or difficulties to your child. A child's sense of self-worth and self-confidence is likely to deepen when adults acknowledge that life has its ups and downs.

> "Our survey research indicated that the majority of young girls are dissatisfied with their appearance. Many believe they are too fat by third or fourth grade. When you have such attitudes at such an early age, you have an increased potential for eating disorders."
>
> —Dr. Arthur Robin
> of Wayne State University, Michigan

INTERACTIONS WITH AUTHORITY FIGURES

YOUR child's teacher may describe your fourth grader by using words such as "pleasant," "agreeable," "a joy to be around." You might agree with that assessment, or you may sit dumbfounded before the teacher, jaw dropped to your chest in disbelief. Is she describing the same child who at home can be bossy, needy, and gives new meaning to the word difficult?

The fourth grade child is an independent thinker, putting previously learned life lessons to the test by making decisions for himself. Sometimes he will make the wrong decisions, and these will manifest themselves in the way he interacts with you. He may think you are wrong about something, and will willingly, and sometimes loudly, explain to you the error of your ways, often in tones that are not becoming of a nine- or ten-year-old child.

These interactions may leave you feeling exasperated, and searching for new methods of interacting with the new person your child is becoming. The way you handle these situations will provide guidance for your child as he learns more about relationships and appropriate behavior. Becoming inflamed and engaging your child in drawn out vocal disputes does nothing but exacerbate the situation. Because you will constantly be put to the test, try becoming more creative in your instruction, and in your interaction with your fourth grader.

Let me prepare you now for the inevitable, "Well, Danny's mom lets him ride his bike to the playground if he wants to!" or "You always make me do chores! None of my friends have to do chores!" If you have not heard similar phrases by now, consider yourself very fortunate, then prepare. Fourth grade children, the social creatures that they are, will not think twice when attempting to use their peer group as a weapon against you. Already angry, they will lash out, subconsciously hoping that you will place as much value on their peer group, and their values, as they do. They will also assume that you are as influenced by your peer group as they are by theirs, hence the comments about Danny's mom.

Now, before you spit out the "If Danny's mom let him jump off a cliff, would you want me to let you do it, too?" rebuttal, take a deep breath. First consider if your child clearly understands the reasoning behind your answer. Has he already been told numerous times that he cannot ride his bike to the park, and been told the reasons why? If so, you might want to remind him to think about why he is not allowed to go, in another room, away from you. You may also invite him to join you when he remembers, and if he does not remember, do try to be patient as you explain it to him, yet again.

If you have not clearly told your child why he is not allowed to go, you might want to tell him. Although he may not like the explanation you offer, he will have a level of understanding of the reasons that you provide. If it is a safety issue, share those concerns with him, using this moment to teach your child some important lessons. If the reason that you don't want him riding to the playground is because you have other plans, explain those plans as well, not necessarily in depth—a simple "Your little brother has a dentist appointment" will suffice. Perhaps you will want to offer a compromise—of course dependent upon your child's change of attitude. Suggest that he meet his friends there tomorrow.

Although it may not be necessary to address at the same time, do you consider what your child is really saying to you? Is he really angry that you won't let him go, or has he already promised his friends that he could go, and does not want to now lose face? Does he have a new bike that he is just dying to show off to his friends? Consider what the real issue is, and while doing so remember that you are setting the rules by which your fourth grader will learn to interact with others. Either way, you will have calmly dealt with the core issue. You will have listened to what your child said, and what he didn't say, and you will have spent a few minutes in logical, reasonable discussion, rather than heated arguing.

You will both walk away from this situation, perhaps still a bit angry and frustrated, but at least a bit more calm than you would have been if you had continued the dispute. Remember, you are laying the groundwork for the teen years, now. The occasionally difficult fourth grader is a practice for the even more obstinate personality of the teenager.

THE TOUGH STUFF: VIOLENCE, INTOLERANCE, AND DRUG ABUSE

Violence

AS your child gets older, she will become more observant of the world around her. Unfortunately her observations will not always be pleasant. In addition to learning about charity, volunteerism, and good citizenship, she will be exposed to the violence and bigotry of today's school environment. A disheartening fact facing today's parent is that school violence has marred the headlines more frequently over the past few years than ever before. Parents are becoming more cautious and concerned about sending their children to school. Formerly considered a warm sunny, safe haven, the local elementary school now is fraught with subtle reminders that the possibility for violence is ever-present.

Although sometimes controversial, many of the nation's schools are making policy and operational modifications to combat violence. Some of these modifications include:

➤ Enforcing zero tolerance policies
➤ Requiring students to wear uniforms
➤ Employing various security measures such as requiring visitor sign-in and using metal detectors
➤ Having police or other law enforcement representatives stationed at the school
➤ Offering students various types of violence prevention programs

You can help your fourth grader's growing awareness and concern about school violence by engaging her frank age-appropriate discussion. It is important to remind her that although there have been many high profile incidents of school violence, the majority of schools can be considered safe. She may then counter that if school is safe, why is there a need for the new security policies. Be calm when reassuring her that these policies are put in place to ensure that her school remains calm and violence-free.

Intolerance

Your fourth grader's increased awareness of the world around him, as well as the new focus on social studies in the classroom, may fill your child with questions and curiosity about others. Questions about a classmate's religion, race, or ethnicity may be posed, possibly catching you off guard. Do your best to provide accurate information, using terminology that is generally considered acceptable. Remember that your child learns from you. Be a good role model. Don't encourage or tolerate bigotry in your home. Avoid using stereotypes in your daily thoughts and communications. Educate yourself and your child about the world and people around you. Today's global community demands that people of all races, religions, and cultures learn to work together.

A sad and difficult situation is when your child finds himself a victim of bigotry or intolerance. He will definitely need your support during these difficult times. Although it may be tempting, do not fight fire with fire. Encourage your child to stand tall, be proud, and to refrain from stooping to a lower level. If your child is having difficulty at school because of bigotry or intolerance, schedule a conference or meeting with school administrators, and your fourth grader's teachers. They need to be made aware of the situation so that they can effectively monitor it, and to be sure that your child is no longer victimized.

Drug Awareness and Abuse

Children in the fourth grade often receive a basic classroom–based education in the areas of drug use and abuse. Unfortunately, many fourth grade children may already have a firsthand real-life education on alcohol and drug abuse; this year, they may become even more familiar. In fact, this year, your child is much more susceptible to drug and alcohol experimentation than ever before. The growing levels of peer pressure, the wavering self-esteem, and the natural curiosity of a fourth grader make this child easy prey for those peddling drugs. Your child may smoke a cigarette on a dare, may take a sip of alcohol from a cabinet out of curiosity, or smoke marijuana in an effort to feel important and grown up.

Curbing this early chemical abuse should be of paramount importance to our society as a whole. Do your part by engaging your child in constructive discussion about the harms of drug and alcohol abuse. Be a good role model. It cannot be said enough times; your child looks to you for guidance. Take that role seriously, guide responsibly. Contact your local health center for information to help you talk to your child about the many temptations that will be facing him in the years to come.

Some of the nation's fourth grade students have already started drinking beer and wine coolers or sniffing inhalants on a monthly basis, according to Parents' Resource Institute for Drug Education. In a self-reported survey of 26,086 fourth-, fifth- and sixth-grade students nationwide, fourth graders said they had used cigarettes (4.1%), beer (7.7%) and inhalants (6.3%) at some time. Of those fourth graders, 2.1% said they drink beer, 2.2% drink wine coolers, and 2.2% use inhalants on a monthly basis.

SUMMARY

FOURTH grade children are not always the most pleasant children. They are frequently unhappy or confused about themselves, and may therefore lash out at the authority figures in their lives. You will need to stow away a vast supply of patience and creativity to draw on when your fourth grader becomes stubborn.

Also, understand that healthy social growth does not mandate that your fourth grader be a social butterfly. He or she may be perfectly happy, enjoying a few quality friendships, and still be considered a very socially adjusted child. Shyness should be understood, and not frowned upon; it is not uncommon for a shy child to spontaneously erupt from his shell, ready to take on the world.

Fourth grade will offer learning vignettes, moments that a parent or teacher can take hold of and teach a child important social lessons. Keep your eyes open for these opportunities. They often present themselves when you least expect it!

While you will undoubtedly be concerned about your child's academic success, and you may place value on your child's physical prowess, it is indeed the ability to interact with others and to grow into a responsible citizen that will set your child apart as an adult. Given the foundation to healthy self esteem, tools for social interaction, and the guidance to make informed, independent decisions, your child will certainly become an asset to the community.

If you are concerned about your fourth grader's social growth, consider the following checklist provided by the Educational Resources Information Center, a service of the U.S. Department of Education. The websites for these resources can be accessed at *www.ed.gov*. Remember that children, just as adults, can be moody, and are not always happy. While this checklist should not be considered a definite indicator of social difficulty, you may notice some social skills that you may want to help your fourth grader develop. Answer the questions in the checklist in a broader sense, noticing trends in your child's behavior.

The Social Attributes Checklist

I. PERSONALITY ATTRIBUTES—The child:
1. Is USUALLY in a positive mood
2. Is not EXCESSIVELY dependent on the teacher, assistant, or other adults
3. USUALLY comes to the program or setting willingly
4. USUALLY copes with rebuffs and reverses adequately
5. Shows the capacity to empathize
6. Has positive relationship with one or two peers; shows capacity to really care about them, miss them if absent, etc.
7. Displays the capacity for humor
8. Does not seem to be acutely or chronically lonely

II. SOCIAL SKILL ATTRIBUTES—The child USUALLY:
1. Approaches others positively
2. Expresses wishes and preferences clearly; gives reasons for actions and positions
3. Asserts own rights and needs appropriately
4. Is not easily intimidated by bullies
5. Expresses frustrations and anger effectively and without harming others or property
6. Gains access to ongoing groups at play and work
7. Enters ongoing discussion on the subject; makes relevant contributions to ongoing activities
8. Takes turns fairly easily

9. Shows interest in others; exchanges information with and requests information from others appropriately
10. Negotiates and compromises with others appropriately
11. Does not draw inappropriate attention to self
12. Accepts and enjoys peers and adults of ethnic groups other than his or her own
13. Interacts non-verbally with other children with smiles, waves, nods, etc.

III. PEER RELATIONSHIP ATTRIBUTES—The child is:
1. USUALLY accepted, not neglected or rejected by other children
2. SOMETIMES invited by other children to join them in play, friendship, and work

6

The 4th Grade
Educational Team

SPRINKLED generously throughout this book, you have found the word "team." As defined by Merriam-Webster, a team is a number of persons associated together in work or activity. To be a member of a team, one must be willing to cooperate with the other members of the group to work toward the common good. In this case, the educational team's paramount purpose is to ensure the educational success of a singular team member, your fourth grader.

Throughout your child's school career, the educational team has changed. Whereas the kindergarten educational team may have only included yourself, your child, and the teacher, this year's team has grown to best fit your child's more specific needs. The current educational team may include a group of teachers, a counselor, perhaps one or more administrators, as well as other support staff such as music and art instructors or tutors. Every member of the team offers a unique perspective on the child, the child's needs, and the activities that can best guarantee future success.

Unfortunately, many parents do not feel as though they are active participants in the educational team. They may find themselves sitting the bench, anxious observers, wanting to join, but not sure when they should jump into the event that is their child's education. To combat this problem, it is of the utmost importance that parents become comfortable with their teammates, and familiar with the rules of the game. As soon as parents feel comfortable with the educational process, they will know when it is best to intervene, and even become the team leader sometimes. Being at ease with the process is productive and empowering.

THE EVENT

A CHILD'S educational process occurs in many venues. Most people envision a classroom when they think of education. This classroom could be in a public school or private school, within an urban or rural community, or in one of many other settings. To think of education in such a way, though accurate, can be very limiting. In reality, a child's education spans the entire day, and all of the events that the child may participate in throughout the day. Whether a child is at home, in the car, on a soccer field, sitting in front of a piano, or is actually standing at the blackboard in the classroom, she is being educated. Within a twenty-four hour day, your child is constantly absorbing the information that will mold the person that she will be tomorrow.

THE TEAM

BEING a member of a team carries with it a set of responsibilities. Each member is expected to carry his or her own weight if the group is to succeed at the task before them. Understanding the roles and responsibilities of each member better equips the parent with the tools necessary to be a child's best advocate.

When my oldest child registered for kindergarten, our school encouraged the parents to meet the teacher and school principal. At this meeting, a month before relinquishing my child to the local school system, I was invited to enter the principal's office. You can imagine how nervous I was to walk into the office with my five-year-old, his small hand folded within my much larger and sweatier palm. A smiling face welcomed me to the office, and welcomed my son to the school. Then, and only then, did I relax the slightest bit. I took a seat and learned a bit about bus schedules, basic rules, and expectations. The principal then inquired, "Do you have any questions or comments?" I paused, and then took a deep breath before I very calmly and respectfully responded, "Yes, I just want you to know how important this little guy is to me, and you will probably get to know me better because I plan to be an active member in his education." Not sure what to expect, I waited. All of my nerves were calmed when the elementary school principal winked at me and said that she was sure that she could agree to those terms. What started out to be a nervous parent meeting the person in charge of the school ended up being the beginning of what is still a wonderful relationship between team members.

Every teacher and administrator consulted and interviewed for this book has conveyed the same wish—for parents to be active participants in their child's education. Studies have shown that providing a supportive team environment helps your child's educational success immensely. Some of the benefits include:

- ➤ Enhanced children's self-esteem
- ➤ Improved children's academic achievement
- ➤ Improved parent-child relationships
- ➤ Parents develop positive attitudes toward school
- ➤ Better understanding of the schooling process

Responsibilities of Parents

Simply remembering that your child has probably spent more time with you since birth than with any other person automatically makes you the expert on your child's personality and inherent skills. This specialized knowledge places you in an important spot on the educational team and other members of the educational team will turn to you. You may notice how enthusiastically they welcome your input, and carefully consider the information and opinions you supply.

Studies published by the U.S. Department of Education have shown that certain attributes contribute to a parent's ability and probability to be involved an involved educational team member. These qualities include: marital happiness, family harmony, success in prior collaborations, and openness to others' ideas. Parents who have high self-esteem are also more likely to have a positive influence on their child's educational success.

Often, parents wait too long to become involved in their child's school life. Not until a disciplinary problem arises, or grades slip almost irrecoverably does this parent visit or have contact with the other members of the team. When called to the school to deal with an academic, behavior or other school issue, the parent becomes apprehensive, unnerved. Because this parent feels out of control with the situation, she may be angry or disgruntled when walking into the unfamiliar school. This parent feels uncomfortable in the surroundings, and may be distant, uncooperative, or timid. A parent exhibiting these emotions has difficulty being a positive and productive team member. Parents, like these, who only become involved in their child's educational success when there is a problem, are said to be "reactive parents." This style of educational participation is usually not conducive to the educational success of the fourth grader. By the time the reactive parent realizes that there is a problem, works with the rest of the team to find solutions, and then implements the plan of action, the child's self-confidence may have deteriorated, thus affecting all aspects of his life.

Another type of parent provides a more positive influence to his child's education; this is the "proactive parent." The pro-active parent is keenly aware of the child's strengths, weaknesses, and needs, whether academic or social. This parent may write a note to the teacher, requesting information or a conference, rather than waiting for a request from the school. When asked to attend a meeting or conference the pro-active parent will arrive confident, prepared and comfortable, ready to discuss the problem at hand. Pro-active parents may also:

> ➤ Visit their child's classroom; a visit will give an idea of what their child does at school and how he interacts with other children.
> ➤ Volunteer to help in the classroom as an assistant (listening to children read, for example, or serving as an aide during computer work).
> ➤ Support student events and performances by helping with them (such as sewing costumes or painting scenery for a school play) and by attending them.
> ➤ If the school has a Parents' Room/Lounge or Parent Center, drop in to meet other parents and teachers there, or to pick up information and materials.
> ➤ Participate in workshops that are offered, such as those on child development or concerns that parents have (or help plan such workshops).

➤ Take advantage of parent-teacher contracts (perhaps agreeing to read with their child for a certain amount of time each night).

➤ Ask their child's teacher if she has materials that can be used to help their child at home and to supplement homework.

➤ Be part of decision-making committees about school issues and problems, such as a Parent Advisory Committee.

➤ Attend parent-teacher conferences and other opportunities for parent-teacher interaction.

You may also want to refer to Chapter 1 for more discussion on parental involvement in a child's education.

Another example of proactive parenting versus reactive parenting can be demonstrated when considering a child who is ill or facing another important life event. The reactive parent may wait until a child has been absent from school for many days or until the school nurse calls before requesting the child's homework. The proactive parent will contact the school, informing the rest of the educational team that the child may miss several days of school, and asking what the child can do to keep on top of things. Keeping your child's educational team updated about important events in your child's life is one example of proactive parenting. The proactive parent will find that teachers will often be more than understanding and amenable if they are kept apprised of any extended illnesses or other crises your child faces.

When emotions are running high, it is sometimes difficult to rely on common sense. Here are a few things parents should keep in mind about teachers.

➤ Teachers are trained professionals. They have the best interest of your child at heart. A teacher would rather hear directly from a parent if there is a problem. Teachers appreciate honest communication, not hearing about problems from another teacher, another parent, or the principal. Teachers are available to have open and informed discussions about your child. Unlike other professionals, teachers deal with 18–22 people at one time, whom they are responsible for all day. If a teacher says she has a concern, most of the time it comes from a genuine concern for your child. Teachers work very hard to manage, get to know, support, and challenge each student individually, as well as being accountable for a lot. This includes everyone's lunch money, missing personal items, as well as what each child is saying and doing to each other child all day long.

➤ Don't let a little problem get to be a big one before you help the teacher solve it. You live with your child. If a teacher requests a conference with you, it is to brainstorm with you and get ideas as to how best to help your child have the maximum success that she can.

➤ Help the teacher help your child. Let your child be as responsible for his things as he can. If you constantly cover for him, always bring forgotten items; always make excuses for his grades or behavior, always take your child's word without giving the teacher a chance or believing what she says, this gives the child the message that it's parents against the teacher instead of the two working as a team — and no one wins. Least of all, your child.

➤ Help your child be at school on time. If she's always late, she's missing a lot. If she's not there, she can't be taught.

Equally helpful are some ideas that an involved parent should remember:

➤ You are the only advocate that your child has. If you have a problem/question with someone/something at school, it is your obligation to your child to find out how you can help them solve it.

➤ You need to be involved in your child's education. Remember that education begins at home. Go to a couple of PTA meetings, always go to open house, and try to take at least one afternoon off to make at least one party or field trip during the year.

You are on a team with the teacher. Your child should always see you as a unified front, working for her best interest. If you have a conflict with the teacher, schedule a conference without your child present to discuss the matter first. Then, if needed, talk with the teacher and your child.

Responsibilities of Teachers

The crux of the educational system, teachers, are on the front lines of the parent-teacher-child relationship. The classroom teacher is the primary contact

THE CHILD AT HOME, THE CHILD AT SCHOOL

The classroom teacher often has a keen understanding of a child's academic strengths and weaknesses, while also observing the social behavior and dynamics within the classroom. The student, child, and citizen that your fourth grader's teacher describes to you may not be the same child you observe at home. Whereas you may have a very social child, one who is constantly talking and laughing at home, your child's teacher may observe the exact opposite. A mom in Pennsylvania was very surprised when a teacher once described her son as reserved and timid.

"He does not take risks."

"He works so well independently; we need to build his group skills."

"I wish we could get him to come out of his shell a bit."

At home he was seeing the exact opposite. He was laughing, joking, playing. He played several team sports, enjoyed scouting, and was constantly in the company of his brother or his friends. And, he never stopped talking! Similar stories are not uncommon. Children often respond differently to the school atmosphere than they do anywhere else. A child who is well behaved at home may be difficult and unruly in the school setting. Likewise, a child who is uncontrollable at home may be a wonderful student—a leader in the classroom. Leaders become followers and followers become leaders. Having a friendly productive rapport with your child's teacher could allow you to view a completely different child than the boy or girl whom you tuck in at night.

for all members of the educational team. Whenever the parent is disturbed about the progress of the educational team, the teacher is the first person questioned. If an administrator has concerns about a particular child, the classroom teacher is consulted. The support staff depends on the classroom teacher for feedback. Most important, the child will spend a significant amount of time with the classroom teacher; the association evident when your fourth grader claims, "I am in Mrs. Jones's class."

Because of this high level of visibility, the teacher will often set the tone for learning this year. You have probably already heard claims of, "she is a strict teacher" or "he gives a lot of homework." These comments are not made nearly so often in reference to anyone else in the educational team. This responsibility not only leads to increased pressure to succeed, but also puts the teacher in the position to be of invaluable assistance to the parent and student. Parents also convey that the following attributes are desirable to provide a collaborative parent-teacher environment: positive attitudes, active planning to involve parents, continuous teacher training, involvement in professional growth, and personal competence.

EFFECTIVE PARENT-TEACHER CONFERENCES

PARENT-TEACHER conferences should never be ignored. This is one of the prime occasions that you will have to get to know your child's teacher. Do not be intimidated by your child's teacher. You are both on the same team, with your child's best interest at heart. You will find that having a respectful, open relationship with your child's teacher alleviates stress that your child may feel at school.

Even if you are aware of no problems with your child, academic or behavioral, you should attend and prepare for these conferences. The parent-teacher conference provides opportunity to interact with the teacher without children present. While you may have an open stream of communication with your child's teacher, the conference will afford you the occasion to have valuable, and sometimes difficult discussion with your teammate.

Addressing Academic Problems

Throughout a child's educational career, there will be a few stumbles, most likely. Almost every child will, at some time, experience some level of academic difficulty. This is one of the common topics discussed at a parent-teacher conference. Some strategies that have proven to be useful when discussing a child's learning problems with the teacher include:

➤ **Consider the context of the problem.**

Ask the teacher to be specific about the problem and the context in which the problem occurs. Children who experience difficulty in learning may do so for many reasons. They may be experiencing frustrations with peers, with family arrangements, or with specific subjects or learning situations. It may be beneficial for teachers to pinpoint both strengths and weaknesses that the child displays. Parents can then work with teachers to identify specific situations in which the difficulty occurs.

➤ **Identify successful strategies.**

Ask the teacher what is being done to help the child overcome the problem. Ideally, the teacher has tried several strategies to help the child overcome the learning problem. Sometimes small steps, such as moving a child to a different place in the room or shortening an assignment, can make a difference. Often children find it difficult to let the teacher know that they do not understand what is expected of them. It may be helpful to have the teacher talk to the child about his or her problem along with the parent.

➤ **Make a plan.**

Ask the teacher about some specifics regarding what can be done to help the child at home. Together with the teacher, the parent can list three or four concrete actions to do every day. It may be as simple as a change in the evening schedule so that the child has 15 to 20 minutes of the parent's time to read together or work on math homework. A regular schedule is usually beneficial to a child. An easily distracted child might benefit from two shorter periods of work rather than one long session. For example, it may be more effective to learn to spell three new words a night than to study 10 or 12 words the night before a test.

➤ **Arrange for follow-up communications.**

Before leaving the conference, it is a good idea to agree with the teacher on what is expected of the child, what the teacher will do to help, and what the parent will do. Sometimes it is helpful to involve the child in these decisions so that he can see that the teacher and parents are working together to help alleviate the problem. A follow-up conference can be used to review the effectiveness of the plan and to formulate a new plan, if necessary. Scheduling another meeting after three to four weeks signals to the child that both parents and teachers are highly interested in taking effective steps to help him achieve success in learning. This strategy can serve to encourage a child who may have become discouraged from repeated experiences of failure early in the school year.

Addressing Behavior Problems

Some of the more difficult problems to address at school are behavioral issues. It is not uncommon for children to act out at some time, and get in trouble in school. During this year of increased peer pressure, your fourth grader may suddenly display less respect for classroom rules. Even the model student may experience brief bouts of behavior problems during the fourth grade. Usually repeated misbehavior, or an unusual change in a child's behavior pattern will result in a conference between the parent and teacher. It is important that all team members attend this meeting with open minds, and with one focus—to solve the problem that is causing the child to act out. Some of important conference tactics include:

➤ **Specify the behavior.**

Ask the teacher to be specific about the type of misbehavior in which the child engages. Aggressive behavior may be a child's way of getting something from a peer rather than of intentionally bringing harm to another person. Inability to follow directions may be a result of a hearing or language problem rather than evidence of direct defiance of the teacher. It is helpful to consider many possibilities when pinpointing the behavior in question.

➤ **Examine the context.**

Ask the teacher to help determine when, where, and why the misbehavior is occurring. Try to identify with the teacher any events that may have contributed to a specific incident of misconduct. Try to take into consideration anything that might be contributing to the situation: the influence of peers, time of day, family problems, illness or fatigue, or changes in schedule or after-school activities. Children may be more prone to misconduct when they are tired or irritable.

➤ **Examine the teacher's expectations.**

Ask the teacher to be as specific as possible about what a child does that is different from what the teacher expects in a particular situation. Sometimes, if the teacher assumes that a child is being intentionally aggressive, the teacher's expectation of aggressive acts can become part of the problem and can lead to a "recursive cycle" in which children come to fulfill the expectations set for them. Try to determine with the teacher if the child is capable of meeting the teacher's positive expectations.

➤ **Make a plan.**

Ask the teacher what can be done by everyone involved to help solve the problem. It may be helpful to have the teacher call you if the problem happens again, in order to discuss possible solutions. Parents and teachers can look together at alternative short-term solutions. Often, fourth graders may not understand what is expected of them in specific situations and may need added explanations and encouragement to meet a teacher's expectations. When young children understand the procedures to follow to complete a task, they may be better able to act without guidance. Knowing what to expect and what is expected of them increases children's ability to monitor their own behavior.

➤ **Plan follow-up communications.**

Children are more likely to be concerned about improving their behavior if they believe their parents care about how they behave. When a parent shows enough concern to try a plan of action and then meet again with the teacher to evaluate its effectiveness, the parent sends a strong message to the child that she is expected to behave at school. It is sometimes beneficial to include the child in the follow-up conference, too, so that the child can make suggestions. Knowing that parents and teachers care enough to meet repeatedly about a problem may be more motivating than any material reward a child is offered.

When There Are No Apparent Problems

At some Parent-Teacher meetings, it may seem that there is very little to discuss, especially when a child is thriving both in and out of the classroom. However, there are some questions a parent can ask to learn more from the teacher. If you think that everything is on track, but still want to know more, here are some helpful questions.

➤ **What does my child do that surprises you?**

This question can reveal to parents what expectations the teacher has for the child. Remember that we mentioned earlier that sometimes a child will behave quite differently at school than at home, so the parent may be surprised, as well.

➤ **What is my child reluctant to do?**

This question may reveal to the parents more about the child's interests and dislikes than about their academic abilities. The question may encourage the teacher to talk to the parent about the child's academic and social preferences.

➤ **What is a goal you would like to see my child achieve?**

This question is a great way to find out what expectations the teacher has for the child. Even well behaved and high-achieving children may benefit from setting goals in areas that need improvement or in which they might excel.

➤ **What can I do at home to support what is being done at school?**

Teachers may not always feel comfortable offering unsolicited advice to parents about what goes on at home, so this question is always appreciated. The question helps create a team feeling. It is also a great opportunity to learn something new you can do for your child.

RESOLVING PARENT-TEACHER CONFLICTS

THERE will be inevitable occasions when parents and teachers will disagree. These disagreements occasionally cause stress for the student because she may feel that she is the reason for the conflict. Some common topics of disagreement include curriculum, assignments, peer relationships, and homework. Just because a parent and teacher disagree does not mean that the child's educational success is destined to fail. It means that the team is having a setback, but with the correct strategies, communication, and procedures, the team can be put back on track.

———

A good listener tries to understand what the other person is saying. In the end he may disagree sharply, but because he disagrees, he wants to know exactly what it is he is disagreeing with.

—KENNETH A. WELLS

Some of these strategies include:

➤ **Know the school policy for addressing parent-teacher disagreements.**

Parents should check school and district policies for handling conflicts or disagreements with teachers and should follow the procedures outlined.

➤ **Use discretion about when and where children or teachers are discussed.**

Resist temptations to discuss individual children or specific teachers in inappropriate public or social situations.

➤ **Talk directly with the teacher about problems.**

Don't rely on third parties to address problems. Discuss things directly with the teacher, either in person or by telephone. It is important to check the facts directly with the teacher before drawing conclusions. If you find the problem goes unresolved, take your issue to other school personnel in the order specified by school policy.

➤ **Avoid criticizing the teacher in front of children.**

Be careful of the message you are sending to your child when you make remarks about the teacher. Criticism may put a young child in a bind over divided loyalties. This confusion and conflict may foster arrogance, defiance, and rudeness toward teachers.

➤ **Choose an appropriate time and place to discuss disagreements.**

Parents should keep in mind that at the end of the day, when both teachers and parents are tired, is probably not the best time for a discussion involving strong feelings. It is always best to find a time when both of you will be prepared for an extended discussion.

Using respect, tact, and grace, most parent-teacher conflicts can be resolved successfully. Ideally these disagreements can be solved without a child being aware that there was a conflict at all. If a parent-teacher conflict requires escalation to the principal/administrator level, be sure to be organized, calm, and prepared. Also be sure to have open ears and an even more open mind. Teachers are human, too.

SUMMARY

REMEMBER that parents and teachers work toward the same goals. Each strives to ensure the success of the student. Occasionally you may feel as though you are on different sides of the fence, but it is important to keep a gate of communication open between you. The student, your child, is an important member of this educational team, although his role is not discussed in depth in this chapter. His social and academic growth throughout this year will be the gauge by which you judge the success of the team as a whole. Using the strategies outlined throughout this book should help minimize misunderstandings and conflicts between the most important role models in your young child's life.

7

The 4th Grade Homework and Assignment Guide

ALTHOUGH it may not be accurate to say that no one likes homework, be assured that most children do not cheer excitedly when their teacher assigns homework. Likewise, parents can become frustrated if they feel that their child's homework is too difficult, or too plentiful. As the parent of a fourth grader, you may feel helpless as your child sits at his workspace, struggling over a mountain of assignments. Parents and children alike begin to dread evenings of math worksheets, reading assignments, and spelling drills.

In third grade, your child began to work more independently, reading from textbooks and then answering a series of context-related questions at the end of the chapter. Perhaps she completed a theme project, drawing a picture of the solar system after taking in a space story in reading class. She may have required your help while she studied spelling words or memorized math facts. Now that she is in fourth grade, she will be expected to complete homework assignments that are similar in nature, as well as perfecting new study skills. Though she will become increasingly independent in her homework tasks, you should remain prepared to lend a helping hand.

You may not enjoy spending your evenings assisting with fourth grade homework, and after a long day of schoolwork, be assured that your fourth grader would rather be playing with friends or relaxing. Everyone, even teachers, realizes that homework is not the most pleasant way to whittle away the evening, but recognizing the many benefits of homework can help you keep your energetic fourth grader on the right track. Lucky is the student who has a teacher who assigns homework that is truly interesting to the students, rather than busywork. If a child finds the assignments interesting or fun, he will be more eager to complete the assignment, and will retain more information. Parents can make homework time more tolerable by supporting their fourth grader and encouraging their child to complete the assigned tasks to the best of their ability. The fourth grade child will benefit by gaining higher grades, better study habits, and a more positive attitude toward studying and learning. The involved parent will also view homework as a window to their child's learning style, curriculum, and level of learning.

"Teaching should be full of ideas, not stuffed with facts."

—AUTHOR UNKNOWN

WHY IS HOMEWORK IMPORTANT?

LOOKING back, it's likely that you do not recall homework as a childhood highlight. Do you remember lying across your bed, staring at your math textbook, wondering if you would ever be able to work division problems? It would seem that humans tend to remember their negative experiences with homework much more than they remember the positive. Forgotten is the sense of pride for correctly completing a worksheet of math facts. Remembered are the tears and tantrums, "I can't do this!" As parents, we need to be aware of our own attitudes toward homework. It is important that we do not project our negative feelings onto our children. Although we may become frustrated with our children's homework assignments, and if watching them struggle may stimulate flashbacks to our own educational hurdles, we must remember why it is important that our children have homework assignments. Many parents exclaim, "They already have had school all day. Why should they work for another hour at home?"

Ongoing research has begun to focus on the relationship between academic achievement and homework. Although the findings over the past decade are mixed about whether homework actually increases academic achievement, many teachers and parents agree that homework develops students' initiative and responsibility and fulfills the expectations of students, parents, and the public. In general, homework assignments have been found to be most helpful if they are carefully planned by the teachers and have a direct meaning to the students.

More children today also have personal difficulties that can be directly associated with a host of problems in school, including the ability to complete homework successfully. These include:

➤ Troubled or unstable home lives
➤ Lack of positive adult role models
➤ A high rate of mobility, found among families who move their children from school to school

According to some researchers, two ways to increase students' opportunities to learn are to increase the amount of time that students have to learn and to expand the amount of content they receive. Homework assignments may foster both these goals. Reforms in education have called for increased homework, and as a result, reports show that students are completing considerably more homework than they did a decade ago. According to the U.S. Department of Education, although there are no stringent guidelines in place, many school districts suggest that children in fourth grade be assigned between fifteen and forty-five minutes worth of homework per school night.

Teachers assign homework for many reasons. Homework can help children:

➤ Practice what they have learned in school
➤ Get ready for the next day's class
➤ Use resources, such as libraries and encyclopedias
➤ Learn things they don't have time to learn in school

Homework can also help children learn good habits and attitudes. Some other reasons for assigning homework in the elementary grades are to:

➤ Teach children the fundamentals of working independently

➤ Encourage self-discipline and responsibility, as assignments provide some youngsters with their first chance to manage time and meet deadlines

Homework, oh homework. I hate you, you stink! I wish I could wash you away down the sink!

—JAMES STEVENSON

COMMON HOMEWORK PROBLEMS AND SOLUTIONS

I really thought that by the fourth grade, my son would remember his homework assignments much better than he does! When he brings his homework home, he completes it with ease. My trouble is that he often forgets his homework, or forgets a textbook that he needs to complete his homework. Sometimes he will bring everything home, but forget what the assignment is. My son is bright, and I often become frustrated and embarrassed by his constant state of forgetfulness. Is there anything that I can do to help him?

Perhaps many of your son's classmates are remembering to take homework assignments and books home, but rest assured that your fourth grader is not the only one who has run through a classic case of the "I Forgots." Keep in mind that fourth graders are very active and energetic creatures. This consistently high level of activity sometimes gets in the way of their responsibilities. Also, remember, your fourth grader is still a child. Although you will want to encourage him to become more responsible for his homework and supplies, be aware that these expectations may be difficult for your son to live up to right now. As he grows and matures, he will gain the skills necessary to organize his homework assignments. Until then, you can help your son become more organized. Provide an assignment tablet or agenda. (Many schools now offer assignment tablets for children to write down their homework assignments. If your school does not offer these assignment books, you might want to consider purchasing one yourself.) These assignment tablets are similar to the daily planners that many business people use. Show your child how to effectively use this book to keep track of assignments, and the instructions associated with them. You may also want to help modify how your child thinks about homework by asking pointed questions daily. Some questions that you may want to ask your fourth grader include:

- ➤ What is your assignment today?
- ➤ Is the assignment clear? (If not, suggest calling the school's homework hotline or a classmate.)
- ➤ When is it due?
- ➤ Do you need special resources (e.g., a trip to the library or access to a computer)?
- ➤ Do you need special supplies (e.g., graph paper or poster board)?
- ➤ Have you started today's assignment? Finished it?
- ➤ Is it a long-term assignment (e.g., a report or science project)?
- ➤ For a major project, would it help to write out the steps or make a schedule?
- ➤ Would a practice test be useful?

After a period of time, your fourth grader will then begin to ask himself these questions, subconsciously, and will be able to prioritize and then complete his tasks.

My fourth grade daughter uses an assignment tablet to keep track of her homework assignments for the day, but we still spend a lot of time on the phone with her classmates as we try to decipher what the notes in the assignment book mean. For instance, if she has work problems from her Math book, she may simply write, "Math, page 137." By the time she gets home, she has forgotten exactly what that means. Does that mean she is to read that page, work some or all of the problems on that page, etc. Help!

Encourage your child to take notes concerning homework assignments in case questions arise later at home. Try to remind your daughter that she needs to not only write down the assignment in her assignment tablet (Math, page 137), but also a little note about the assignment. Perhaps something like: *Math, page 137. Work all odd problems, showing all work. Neatness counts.* Notes like this not only give her the actual assignment, but also give her enough information about the assignment so that she will know exactly what is expected of her. She will need help learning to take accurate notes about her homework assignments. Perhaps you could help her by giving her examples, and be sure to praise her when she brings home complete notes about her assignments!

The teacher has informed us that some of my daughter's grade is based on her homework. Does that mean I should correct her homework before she turns it in?

You should check with your child's teacher to see what she expects. The fact that part of her grade is comprised of her homework does not necessarily mean it has to do with the assignment being perfect. Often, the successful completion and submission of the homework is what is being graded. If your child consistently forgets to complete assignments or doesn't hand in her work, this could adversely affect her grade. In either case, the rule of thumb is "Don't do the assignment yourself. It's not your homework—it's your child's." Of course, if your child has questions about her homework, feel free to help explain the question, and help her think through the problem, coming to her own conclusions. If her conclusion is obviously incorrect, help her think through it again, offering some of your own insights. No matter what grade your child is in, ask to look at homework once it has been marked and returned. As always, feel free to ask your child's teachers about their homework policy and specific assignments. How closely you watch over homework will depend on the age of your child, how independent she is, and how well she does in school. Some ways that you can give your fourth grader some gentle guidance are:

➤ Ask what the teacher expects. At the start of the school year, find out what kinds of assignments will be given and how the teacher wants you involved. Some teachers only want you to make sure the assignment is completed. Others want parents to go over the homework and point out mistakes.

➤ Check to see that assignments are started and finished on time. If you aren't home when the homework is finished, look it over when you get home.

➤ Monitor TV viewing and other activities. Homework is done best when the television is off. See that things like choir or basketball don't take too much time. If homework isn't getting done, your child may need to drop an activity.

I know that many parents spend a lot of time helping their children with homework at night. I try to let my children do their homework on their own. How much help should I provide to my fourth grader when doing homework?

As you might imagine, younger children need more parental assistance with homework than older children. As your children get older, your interaction will wane. For now, you should go over homework assignments with your child, carefully reading the instructions together. This will ensure that your child is clear about what is expected of him, and you are kept informed about what he is covering in school. If your child is still unclear about the assignment, do several problems or questions together, then observe your child doing the next one or two. If all seems well, you should encourage him to complete the assignment on his own, allowing him to think through even the more difficult problems. Be sure that he knows that you are available to help him if he has trouble with any of the questions. Although you may be tempted to work a problem as an example for your child, keep in mind that you should help him think through a problem, rather than to just give him the answers.

Last night my fourth grader came to me and told me about a special project that needed to be completed by today. The assignment included a model of a historical icon, such as the Statue of Liberty, White House, or the Liberty Bell. I couldn't believe it! How could the teacher expect a project like that to be completed in only a day? Then I found out the rest of the story. This project had been assigned weeks ago, and my fourth grader had procrastinated! Let's just hope that the glue held on the Popsicle stick Washington Monument that was sent to school today. How can I avoid a repeat performance of this fiasco?

I have been in your shoes before! It is very frustrating, isn't it? With fourth grade comes the introduction of the long-term project; the project that will include often include research, visual models, and an oral or written report. Because the long-term project is a new concept for your fourth grader, he will need your help in breaking the large project into small pieces, and treating each piece as an individual, small project.

For example, one of my children was given a project similar to the one you described. He chose to create a model of a Native American long house. The first small assignment of the larger project is to organize the project into small manageable mini-projects. We did that, and then put the project away for the evening. The next night we began the first "mini-project." For several nights we did research, one night on the Internet, another night at the library. I gave my son index cards to record his research. Each index card was to hold one fact about the Native Americans that would have resided in the long house that we still needed to build. When the weekend came, we marched to the woods to find the bark and sticks that we would use to build our long house. The entire family joined in this part of the assignment; in fact, it did not even feel like homework as we enjoyed the family time together. By the end of the weekend, we had the long house built. Because we still had several days until the project's due date, my son was now able to sit down and write the accompanying report. He organized his index cards into a logical sequence and simply wrote his report from the snippets of information gleaned during his research. The night before the project was due, we packed everything up, making sure that the long house model would survive the trip to school, and *voilà*, we were done!

Long-term projects will frequently be assigned throughout your child's educational career. Your child will benefit from learning how to organize and prioritize these major projects. Here are some tips:

➤ Before doing any real work on the project, create an action plan. Decide how you are going to break the project into mini-projects.

➤ Supply tools, such as index cards or folders, that will help your child focus on each mini-project, rather than becoming overwhelmed on the larger assignment.

➤ If there is a craft portion of the project, try to save that for a weekend. Getting dirty together on a Saturday afternoon seems a lot more fun, and a lot less like homework, than trying to slap something together before bath time during the week.

➤ Keep your child's homework and learning personalities in mind as you plan the project. For example, if your fourth grader is quiet, you may want to plan an evening where she can present her oral report to you.

As soon as my children get home from school, they are expected to do their homework. My fourth grade daughter rushes through her homework. I often have to have her sit back down to re-write, or re-work her problems. How can I help her slow down and take more time with her homework?

Perhaps it is time to evaluate your daughter's homework personality. A child who is doing homework just to get it done isn't able to recognize the importance of the quality of the work. Perhaps she is rushing because she would rather be outdoors playing, or watching her favorite program. You may want to try to give her a small break, perhaps let her have a snack and some playtime. She could then work on her homework after dinner, while you are cleaning up the kitchen.

Parents should understand that all children have their own unique homework personality. For example, I have two sons who have vastly differing homework personalities. My eldest son prefers to start into his homework right after walking in the door and grabbing a snack. My younger son needs to debrief after school. He often plays until dinnertime. After dinner, he sets to work on his homework. While the older child is able to do his homework privately, without supervision, his younger brother needs a homework center in the middle of the house, where he is easily supervised, and finds help easily accessible. Some other things to keep in mind are:

➤ Figure out how your child learns best. Knowing this makes it easier for you to help your child. For example, if your child learns things best when he can see them, draw a picture or a chart to help with some assignments. But if your child learns best when he can handle things, an apple cut four ways can help him learn fractions. If you've never thought about his learning style, observe your child; check with the teacher if you aren't sure.

➤ Encourage good study habits. See that your child schedules enough time for assignments and makes his own practice tests at home, before a test. When a big research report is coming up, encourage him to use the library.

➤ Talk about assignments and ask questions. This helps your child think through an assignment and break it into small, workable parts. For example, ask if she understands the assignment, whether she needs help with the work, and if her answer makes sense to her.

➤ Give praise. People of all ages like to be told when they have done a good job. And give helpful criticism when your child hasn't done his best work so that he can improve.

I hated homework as a child, and admittedly my entire school career suffered because of my refusal to buckle down and put forth my best effort. What can I do to help my fourth grader have a good homework experience?

You are already on the right track! You have identified some key feelings that you had about homework, and have seen the effect of your less-than-stellar efforts on your education. Simply identifying those things about yourself puts you in a wonderful position to help your fourth grader have a successful educational career. One of the most effective things that you can now do for your fourth grader is to express that you think education and homework are important. Children are more eager to do homework if they know their parents care that it gets done. Some helpful tips to ensure that you are setting the right homework tone in your house are:

➤ Set a regular time for homework. The best time is one that works for your child and your family.

➤ Pick a place to study that is fairly quiet and has lots of light. A desk is nice. But the kitchen table or a corner of the living room can work just fine.

➤ Help your child concentrate by turning off the TV and saying no to telephone calls during homework time. If you live in a small or noisy household, have all family members take part in a quiet activity during homework time. You may need to take a noisy toddler outside to play or into another room.

➤ Collect papers, books, pencils, and other things your child needs. Tell the teacher, school counselor, or principal if you need help getting your child these things.

➤ Set a good example by reading and writing yourself. Your child learns what things are important by watching what you do. Encourage educational activities. Go on walks in the neighborhood, trips to the zoo, and encourage chores that teach responsibility.

➤ Read with your child. This activity stimulates interest in reading and language and lays the foundation for your child to become a lifelong reader.

➤ Take your child to the library and encourage him to check out materials needed for homework. Talk about school and learning activities. Attend school activities, such as parent-teacher meetings and sports events.

How can I help my fourth grader with his homework when I don't understand it?

There is nothing that can make a parent feel more helpless than to be unable to help their child with an assignment that they are struggling to complete. Setting the tone for your child's homework career does not mean that you will necessarily know how to do the work assigned to your child. What it does mean is that you will, even when you are at a loss, do your best to locate the correct resources that will be of valuable assistance to your child. I often think of my childhood, when my parents cried out the evils of "New Math." Unfamiliar with the methodologies being taught in the classroom, my parents were able to solve the math problems, but not using the processes that were suggested in the classroom. Not understanding the homework, or the expectations of the teacher, often frustrate not only the student, but also the parent.

If you find yourself holding your head in your hands, equally discouraged about the homework assignment that your fourth grader is trying to complete, think outside of the box. If you are unable to solve the problem, ask for help. There is no shame in calling a friend, talking to other parents whose children may have had a similar assignment, or having your child call a classmate for help. If your child's teacher makes herself available by providing a phone number or e-mail address, contact her. Feel free to ask for clarification of the assignment. If nothing else, she will know that you and your child have made every attempt to complete the assignment. If the project is a long-term project, simply write a note to your child's teacher. Remember, the teacher is a part of the educational team. Your child's success is dependent on the willingness of the entire team to put forth a stellar effort. Because you are teammates, and have already entered into a cooperative relationship, the entire team wins with this sort of collaboration!

My son will be starting fourth grade in the fall. I have heard that there are higher expectations in fourth grade. I do not want him to be stressed. I want him to have the correct tools to be able to successfully complete the most common homework assignments. What sort of supplies should we have at home to help him with his homework?

First, I can tell that your son already has one of the most important supplies—he has a parent who takes a positive and pro-active stance to education.

Armed with that one supply, his chances of educational success are greatly augmented. Yes, your fourth grader will discover that the fourth grade expectations are higher on many levels. Teachers expect a fourth grade student to gradually become more responsible, more conscientious, and of course more knowledgeable. Your fourth grader will also be expected to work more independently than ever before and to do that he will need some tools. Some of the things that you will want to provide for your child are:

➤ A quiet place to work with good light
➤ A regular time each day for doing homework
➤ Basic supplies, including paper, pencils, pens, markers, glue, and a ruler
➤ If possible, access to research tools such as a computer, set of encyclopedias, dictionary, and other tools that could help with special projects

You may have to take a shopping trip to the local craft or department store if your child is working on a special project, such as a model of the solar system, to buy special, one time only, supplies.

How much homework should I expect my fourth grader to have? My daughter spends a lot of time on homework every night. Typically we spend more than an hour a night on homework. Sometimes she completes the assignments on her own, but often I also have to sit with her to help. This has led to a lot of frustration around our house!

As mentioned earlier in this chapter, you should expect your fourth grader to have no more than 45 minutes of homework a night. You will want to evaluate some things about your daughter's nightly homework load. First, it is wonderful that you are trying to support her by being ever-present during her studies. This sets the tone, showing her that you believe that homework is important. Consider also if her homework is excessive, or is most of her time spent daydreaming, glancing up at the television, or just getting herself organized to begin the assignment? Similar to how we grownups track our budget by writing down each and every expense, down to a pack of gum, you will want to keep track of the time your daughter spends on homework, to be sure that indeed the entire hour is spent on homework, and not other superfluous activities.

If, after you have monitored your daughter's homework time, you still believe that the problem is that she has too much homework, you should consider sharing any concerns you may have regarding the amount or type of homework assigned with your child's teacher or principal.

If your child is having trouble with homework:

➤ Call or meet with the teacher. For example, get in touch with the teacher if your child refuses to do assignments, or if you or your child can't understand the instructions, or if you can't help your child get organized to do the assignments.

➤ Believe that the school and the teacher want to help you and your child. Work together to fix or lessen the homework problem. Different problems require different solutions. For example:

■ Does your child have a hard time finishing assignments on time? Perhaps he has poor study skills and needs help getting organized.

■ Is the homework too hard? Maybe your child has fallen behind and needs special help from a teacher or a tutor.

■ Is she bored with the homework? Perhaps it's too easy and your child needs extra assignments that give more challenge. Or perhaps she would be more interested if another way could be found for her to learn the same material. Remember that not all homework can be expected to interest your child. Most teachers, however, want to give homework that children enjoy and can finish successfully, and they welcome comments from parents.

➤ Check with the teacher and with your child to make sure the plan is working.

My son is involved in several after school activities. He takes part in Cub Scouts, sports, and he takes piano lessons. These activities often start right after school. By the time we get home from his activities, and have dinner, it is time for a bath and bedtime. We often complete homework quickly at the end of the night, or in between activities. Is there a good way to balance activities and homework?

Nowadays children are more active in social, athletic, and religious activities than ever before. While these activities are very important and beneficial to a child's growth, it is important to reinforce the importance of school and the need for moderation with extra-curricular activities. Fourth grade children, while extremely energetic, can't sustain a busy schedule every single day. For these reasons, you should consider limiting after-school activities to allow time for both homework and family activities. Talk to your child about which activity is most important to him. Perhaps you can set guidelines for your child to be involved in one sport or activity at a time. Remember, you are trying to build a well-rounded successful person, and he needs to know that his schoolwork is very important, not just something that can be worked in around all the other activities in his life.

HELPING YOUR CHILD WITH HOMEWORK

WHILE you may struggle trying to keep an open and positive attitude about homework while watching your fourth grader struggle night after night, there is help. The U.S. Department of Education has identified four major keys to homework success. By simply including a dose of common sense, mixed with generous participation, and sprinkled with plenty of attention on your part, you will find that these rules will greatly improve the homework scene around your house.

Show That You Think Education and Homework Are Important

What better example can you provide for your fourth grader than to actively voice your opinion that education and schoolwork are important? By simply being a good role model, you will be instrumental in your child's development of a healthier attitude about homework and school in general. Providing the proper tools and environment for learning is just one small way to project the extreme importance of homework. Remember that routine and proper tools are necessary for a child to feel successful. Don't allow yourself to become mired in the thought that a proper homework environment consists of a desk in the corner of the house. Although a desk in a quiet corner often works well as a homework center, the kitchen table or corner of the living room can also work just as well. Some other questions you might want to ask yourself are:

➤ Do you set a regular time every day for homework?
➤ Does your child have the papers, books, pencils, and other things needed to do assignments?
➤ Does your child have a fairly quiet place to study with lots of light?
➤ Do you set a good example by reading and writing yourself?
➤ Do you stay in touch with your child's teachers?

Monitor Assignments

Be a proactive member of the educational team by actively monitoring your child's homework. Too many parents believe that their child is doing well in school, only to be surprised when a teacher sends home an unfavorable progress report. Diligently monitor your fourth grader's homework. Remember that this suddenly independent fourth grader still needs your supervision. Studies have proven that children are more likely to complete assignments if their parents monitor homework. Be available at homework time, offering gentle reminders, when necessary, to keep your fourth grader on track! He is a very active child, both mentally and physically and may need you to help him stay on task. Be aware of feedback from his teacher, your fellow educational team member. Her comments on corrected homework assignments will help guide you and your fourth grader toward the path to success. Under your watch, he will receive help with subjects he is struggling with, and praise for a job well done! Consider the following:

➤ Do you know what your child's homework assignments are? How long they should take? How the teacher wants you to be involved?
➤ Do you see that assignments are started and completed?
➤ Do you read the teacher's comments on assignments that are returned?
➤ Is TV viewing cutting into your child's homework time?

Provide Guidance

Your fellow team member, the teacher, is going to depend on you to help provide the educational lead at home. Your fourth grader will also take cues from you, learning and understanding what your goals are for homework completion. Your fourth grader knows the rules. She has spent several years with teachers who provided guidance on everything from when bathroom breaks were appropriate to how class work papers should be formatted. Even with this knowledge of expectations, the typical physically and mentally active fourth grader may need some gentle nudging and convincing to stay on task. Keep in mind that your child's teacher spends the day teaching children who display a wide variety of learning styles and abilities. You provide your child with the unique situation of providing the exact type of attention that she needs. Because you know your child best, you will be equipped to give her the one-on-one tailored assistance with homework that she probably does not receive at school. Also, you will need to provide firm but gentle rules about how homework is to be completed, where it is to be completed, and when it is to be completed. Parental guidance with homework has become more necessary as many teachers are assigning the tasks for the entire week at the beginning of the week, allowing the parent and child to work at their own pace.

➤ Do you understand and respect your child's style of learning? Does he work better alone or with someone else? Does he learn best when he can see things, hear them, or handle them?

➤ Do you help your child to get organized? Does your child need a calendar or assignment book? A bag for books and a folder for papers?

➤ Do you encourage your child to develop good study habits (e.g., scheduling enough time for big assignments; making up practice tests)?

➤ Do you talk with your child about homework assignments? Does she understand them?

Talk With Someone at School When Problems Come Up

Never forget that you are your child's best advocate. Parents are often the first to notice problems with their child's education. Because you have remained involved and proactive, you will be ready to meet these problems head on. The time that you have spent to nurture a respectful and comfortable relationship with your fellow team members will pay off now as you may need to engage in discussions with your child's teachers. Do not hesitate to make your fourth grader's teacher aware of issues that you or your child may have with the content, frequency, or quantity of homework. Having an open relationship with the teachers and administrators also will give you a clear view of the school's homework policies. Consider the following:

> ➤ Do you meet the teacher early in the year *before* any problems arise?
> ➤ If a problem comes up, do you meet with the teacher?
> ➤ Do you cooperate with the teacher and your child to work out a plan and a schedule to fix homework problems?
> ➤ Do you follow up with the teacher and with your child to make sure the plan is working?

SUMMARY

IN a perfect world, all parents and children would be able to face homework assignments with a smiling face, armed with a plate of healthy snacks. Let's face it, most families would love that, but reality has a way of rearing its sometimes-ugly head. As parents, the best that we can do is to search out resources to help us better organize and educate ourselves, thereby benefiting the blossoming minds within our children. Although the guidelines listed above are not a cure-all, following them can greatly affect the homework attitudes at your house.

Do not fool yourself into believing that being an involved parent is going to transform your child into a homework-loving scholar. Simply strive to raise children who view homework as a necessary part of the complete learning experience. Help your children understand the benefits of homework, even if they don't enjoy it. Remind yourself and your child that homework is a tool used to support the daily lessons learned in the classroom.

Be sure to supply your child with all the supplies necessary to do their job. Imagine if you were expected to show up at your job as a doctor, only to find that you did not have some of the basic tools of your profession, such as a stethoscope. Obviously you would become very frustrated, and perhaps you would begin to develop a negative attitude toward work. Remember that your child's homework is his job; not having the correct supplies to do the job at hand will undoubtedly provoke the same negative reactions in your child.

It is also very advantageous to make time to take your child to the library to check out materials needed for homework, and read with your child as often as you can. Talk about school and learning activities in family conversations. Ask your child what was discussed in class that day. If he doesn't have much to say, try another approach. For example, ask your child to read aloud a story he wrote or discuss the results of a science experiment. Asking pointed questions in a non-threatening way, will often encourage a child to focus on the highlights or low points of his day. Talking to your child opens the doors to understanding.

I cannot overstate how important it is to the child that a parent faces homework with a positive attitude. Take the time to explore and understand your child's homework personality, and make homework into a serene time that you and your child can share within the chaos of your hustle and bustle.

WRAPPING IT UP

OVER the course of this book, we have covered a wide array of material. Hopefully you have been provided with an overview of what to expect of your fourth grader, your fourth grader's teacher, and of yourself during this transition year.

While it is easy to research statistics and facts, then to organize them into a wonderful resource for parents, it is impossible to find a child who neatly fits into all of the statistical matrices provided by scientists, educators, parenting experts, and even authors like myself. That is why I cannot stress enough that you should "trust your gut." You know your child, you know your child's experiences, you know your child's strengths, and if you think about it long enough, you can even identify some weaknesses. You have the advantage!

Consider if you will, how valuable that knowledge is to the others who interact with your fourth grader. Have you ever seen a football coach who does not share the playbook with his quarterback? Does a dance teacher keep to herself the proper ballet positions? Share the playbook! Lead the rest of the educational team in the dance!

Do remember that football coaches continue to study and modify the playbook, and dance instructors continue dancing and exercising. Continue to be involved in your child's education, being aware of new obstacles that may present themselves, and effectively communicating those findings with the rest of the team.

While your child's educational success remains an important facet of this year, you and your fourth grader may begin to embark on a new path of communication. Instead of favorite games and toys, tough topics such as puberty and drug abuse may be fodder for evening conversation. Both you and your child may be a bit uncomfortable as you trip over the words necessary when discussing these difficult topics, but those nervous stutters will eventually be replaced with meaningful frank interactions—and those interactions will be cherished forever! Long after your fourth grader graduates high school, and later college, she will remember the time you spent to talk, to listen, and to love.

Love your children. Enjoy your moments. Cherish them both.

Resources:

The Best "Stuff" for 4th Graders

AS your child gets older, he will be developing his own tastes, but you will still need to be there to encourage his interests. To make that task a little easier, we have compiled a list of the best CD-ROMs, books, magazines, and websites for your child. These are arranged by subject, and sometimes by category. Remember, this is only a sample of the many great resources available, and keep in mind your child's preferences.

CD-ROMs

NOT all parents are familiar with computers or how much technology improves daily. Thankfully, you and your child can benefit from these advances. CD-ROMs are a great alternative to video games, the Internet, and television. The materials found on CD-ROM are multimedia, your child will be able to see pictures, watch videos, and listen to recordings. Below are some of the best CD-ROMs we have found. They are arranged by subject and the age range on most of the following products is 9–12, which means these are products your child may enjoy for years to come.

Reading/Language Arts

Hoyle Word Games
  With 8 games such as crosswords, word searches, and hangman, this interactive CD-ROM is a great way to improve your child's handling of the English language. Cost: $29.99

Reading Blaster 4th Grade

This interactive program offers a fun but educational way to practice grammar, vocabulary, and sentence structure. Cost: $19.99

Scrabble 2

A favorite board game gets updated as a computer program. There are different levels of difficulty, and it can be played with others or against the program's artificial opponent. This is a great way to practice spelling and increase vocabulary. Cost: $29.99

Foreign Language

Rosetta Stone: Spanish Explorer

This CD-ROM is meant to give your child interactive experience with speaking another language. It features native speakers, and the instruction can be customized to your child's learning style. This program is available in several different languages. Cost: $19.99

Smart Start Italian Deluxe

Inspire your child to learn *italiano* with this step-by-step software. There are sample conversations, as well as the most common words and phrases. Cost: $29.99

Social Studies

Where in the World Is Carmen Sandiego?

Carmen Sandiego is a great way to practice geography and learn about the world. There are photos and videos, as well as a foreign language feature. This is a great way to inspire children. Cost: $19.99

My First Amazing World Explorer

Learn about the people and animals of countries around the globe with this program. There are games about capitals, flags, and continents to keep your child interested for hours. Cost: $19.99

History of the World 2.0

This is a great source for articles, biographies, and historical background information. History comes alive with this software. Cost: $24.99

Math

ClueFinders Math 9–12
ClueFinders software covers all grades and subject matters, but in this case, math is the focus for your child. Cost: $15.99

Leap Ahead! Math
This CD-ROM is great for practicing addition, subtraction, multiplication, and division skills. Counting money, telling time, and identifying patterns are also included in this comprehensive package. Cost: $24.99

Science

Human Body Activity Pack
If you have a budding scientist on your hands, this is a fantastic program to own. Mr. Skinless is available for challenging games as well as a unique tour through the human body. Cost: $19.99

I Love Science
This CD-ROM has been designed to pique the interest of seven to eleven year olds, which guarantees that your child can use this program beyond the fourth grade. There are fun facts, experiments, and exciting visuals to keep children interested. Cost: $19.99

A World of Dinosaurs
Children who take an interest in science are sure to love this program. There is a dinosaur adventure, as well as a museum. This is a great way to spark interest for those who may be hesitant to consider science a favorite subject. Cost: $19.99

Arts

Kid Pix Studio Deluxe
Foster your child's creativity with this multimedia tool. Your child will be able to draw, paint, and even animate with this software. Cost: $39.99

Crayola Creativity Pack Print Factory and Make a Masterpiece
Using a variety of tools, your child is encouraged to make his own masterpiece. There are reading and writing activities as well as plenty of creative activities. Cost: $26.99

Other Skills

All Star Typing 9–12
With the explosion of computer use, good typing skills are not just reserved for the office. Give your child a head start in learning proper technique; later your child will build speed and increase accuracy. Cost: $29.95

My First Amazing Diary
Encourage your child to write! With this CD-ROM your child can indulge in some creative writing or use it as a means of thoughtful self-expression. Cost: $19.99

OLDER READER BOOKS

BY the fourth grade, the daunting task of learning to read has been accomplished. The harder task now is to keep your child reading every day. We have chosen some books that are popular for fourth graders, some are classics, others are new favorites and award winners. The reading level varies among these titles, so make sure that it is not too challenging or too easy. Most important your child should read what she likes, that is the key to sustaining a lifetime reader.

Arthur: The Seeing Stone, by Kevin Crossley-Holland (Orion, 2000)
Black Beauty, by Anna Sewell (Avon, 1997)
Bridge to Terabithia, by Katherine Paterson (HarperCollins, 1978)
Bud, Not Buddy, by Christopher Paul Curtis (Delacorte, 1999)
Charlie and the Chocolate Factory, by Roald Dahl (Knopf, 1985)
Charlotte's Web, by E.B. White (HarperCollins, 1987)
Harry Potter series, by J.K. Rowling (Scholastic, 1998)
Little Women, by Louisa May Alcott (Price Stern Sloan, 1983)

Tales of a Fourth Grade Nothing, by Judy Blume (EP Dutton, 1972)
The Other Side of Truth, by Beverly Naidoo (Puffin, 2000)
The Phantom Tollbooth, by Norton Juster (Random House, 1988)
The Wind in the Willows, by Kenneth Grahame (Henry Holt, 1980)
The Wind Singer, by William Nicholson (Mammoth, 2000)
Where the Red Fern Grows, by Wilson Rawls (Bantam Starfire, 1984)
Where the Sidewalk Ends, by Shel Silverstein (HarperCollins, 1974)

Language Arts

The Journey of English, by Donna Brook (Clarion, 1998)
Shakespeare Stories, by Leon Garfield (Houghton Mifflin, 1991)

Foreign Language

Goodbye USA: Bonjour La France, by Anne Elizabeth Bovaird (Barrons, 1993)
Pen Pals: A Friendship in Spanish and English, by Catherine Bruzzone (NTC, 1998)

Science

3D Eyewitness: Human Body, by Richard Walker (DK, 1999)
The Way Things Work Kit, by David Macaulay (DK, 2000)

Math

Cool Math: Math Tricks, Awesome Math Factoids, and More, by Christy Magazini (Price Stern Sloan, 1997)
Everything You Need to Know About Math Homework, by Anne Zeman (Scholastic, 1994)

Social Studies

100 Natural Wonders of the World, by Bill Yenne (Bluewood, 1995)
Marie Antoinette: Princess of Versailles, by Kathryn Lasky (Scholastic, 2000)

Computers

101 Things to Do with Your Computer, by Gillian Doherty (EDC, 1998)
Make Your Own Web Page!, by Ted Pedersen (Price Stern Sloan, 1998)

Arts

The Barefoot Book of Stories from the Opera, by Shahrukh Husain (Barefoot, 1999)
Young Person's Guide to Music, by Neil Ardley (DK, 1995)

MAGAZINES

CHILDREN love to receive mail, so pair that with their love of reading, and there is no reason not to indulge in a magazine subscription. There are magazines for every interest and at reasonable prices. Here are a few of the best we found.

Boys' Life
For boys aged 7 through 17, this is a great general interest magazine.
Contact Kids
This is a technology and science must-have! Geared at children 9–12, there are articles, games, experiments, and reviews.
Creative Kids
Appropriately named, this magazine for 8–14 year olds is meant to encourage creativity.
Cricket
For readers 9–14 this is a general interest magazine with stories, recipes, science articles, and games.

Dig

> *Dig* is perfect for a budding archaeology. Mummies, dinosaurs, and ancient civilizations fill the pages of this magazine for 8–13 year olds.

Girls' Life

> For girls 8 through 14, this magazine has plenty of advice, stories, celebrity interviews, and other topics of interest.

Kid's Wall Street News

> This magazine is a great introduction to saving, investing, and learning about the economy. This new magazine is for those 8 and up.

National Geographic World

> With great articles about wildlife and world cultures, this award–winning magazine is perfect for children 8 and up.

Nickelodeon

> This is an entertainment magazine by the children's television network by the same name. There are puzzles, celebrity interviews, and comics.

WEBSITES

AT the time of publication, the websites listed here were current. Due to the ever-changing nature of the web, we cannot guarantee their continued existence or content. Parents should always supervise their children while they are on the Internet.

Below you will find several websites that have been categorized by their purpose.

> If you have concerns and you would like to know more about Internet safety, visit the FBI's site "A Parent's Guide to Internet Safety," at *www.fbi.gov/library/pguide/pguide.htm;* or you can try *www.ed.gov/pubs/parents/internet* for "Parents Guide to the Internet," which is hosted by the U.S. Department of Education.

Homework Help

Are you looking for a way to make homework more interesting? Visit these great sites with your child to find materials to help your child with his work.

www.bjpinchbeck.com

This site, now hosted on *Discovery.com*, was created by B.J. and his father. This is a great portal to hundreds of sites dedicated to helping students complete their homework, and to learn something new.

www.bigchalk.com

Formerly *HomeworkCentral.com*, *BigChalk* now encompasses resources for students, parents, and teachers. If your child needs help with homework, he can find help that is both grade and subject specific.

Reference Guides

In fourth grade your child will be asked to complete assignments that require some research. The Internet is a great place to gain access to excellent reference sites, such as the ones listed below.

www.brittanica.com

This site offers free access to Britannica Encyclopaedias as well as a wealth of other new reference sites.

http://kids.infoplease.com

At *Infoplease*, students not only have access to a homework center, but there is a variety of almanacs, dictionaries, and encyclopedias.

"Edutainment"

By "edutainment," we mean sites that are both educational and entertaining. The goal is that your child will be learning without even knowing it. There are literally hundreds of thousands of great sites for your child to explore. We have tried to bring you a few of the best that not only have great content, but also have excellent links to other sites.

www.crayola.com

The people at Crayola offer a site full of crafts for kids. There is a game room, coloring books, craft suggestions, and stories.

www.exploratorium.edu

The famous San Francisco museum by the same name hosts this site. The museum is dedicated to science, art, and human perception. Here you will find exhibitions from the museum, activities, and resources for projects.

www.funschool.com

Funschool promises regularly updated educational content for children. Click on "Third & Fourth Grade" from the homepage for excellent content developed especially for your child's age level.

http://kids.msfc.nasa.gov

NASA is sure to find some new recruits for the space program from this site! Complete with space art, space stories, and games, this site will keep children captivated for hours.

www.nick.com

This site comes from the folks at Nickelodeon. While much of this site is dedicated to their programming, there are other pages that offer more of a challenge. Go to "Noggin" from the home page to find games and fun facts for children.

http://nyelabs.kcts.org

A must for the budding scientist! *Bill Nye, The Science Guy* has created a site that is a lot of fun for kids. It is loaded with fun and interesting facts and lots of fun and safe science projects to do at home.

www.pbs.org

PBS has a great site for kids, parents, and teachers alike. Head to PBS KIDS from the home page and be astonished by the quality and quantity of content. Colorful and filled with all your favorite characters, this site is a MUST for parents and kids.

TELEVISION PROGRAMMING

If you are like most households in the United States, you are watching dozens of hours of television every week. Here are some helpful hints:

1. Avoid programs that are geared exclusively toward selling a product.
2. Find programs that have a message, either moral or educational.
3. Talk with your child after watching a program. Discuss the events of the story, how the characters behaved, you can even talk about the commercials they showed.
4. Steer your child to programming that challenges him to think, feel, or communicate. Television should not be time to vegetate.
5. Seek programming that is both educational and entertaining. Believe it or not, there are quality programs out there.

Some stations that have plenty of educational programming for children are Animal Planet, The Discovery Channel, The History Channel, The Learning Channel, PBS, and The Travel Channel.

www.surfmonkey.com

The content on this site is sure to please your fourth grader. Their wonderful links are organized by categories such as playful, artsy, brainy, spacey, newsworthy, techie, worldly, and starstruck.

www.worldbook.com

Head straight for World Book's Fun and Learning page. There you will find games, news and even a Cyber Camp complete with a summer's worth of activities.

www.yahooligans.com

From the creators of Yahoo, comes *Yahooligans*, a web guide designed for children. Topics included are sports, around the world, and arts and entertainment.

FOR PARENTS

Websites

THERE is a lot to know about your child and her education. For this reason, we would like to offer websites that have content that is both informative and interactive. You can not only read articles about topics of interest, but you can post your own ideas, and ask questions from the experts.

www.about.com

This site, although not dedicated to education and parenting, has a wealth of links on these subjects. The experts at *about.com* are also there to answer your questions.

www.bigchalk.com

This site is a great resource not only for parents and children, but also for teachers and educators. You can search by subject, grade level, as well as by topic.

www.childfun.com

This site has plenty of tips and resources for parents on every topic as well as a free newsletter with plenty of great ideas for activities for your child.

www.ed.gov

The U.S. Department of Education hosts this site to present accurate and complete information to parents regarding education in the United States.

www.edu4kids.com

The content on this site is great for parents looking to provide their children with quality, cost-free learning activities in the major subjects.

www.familyeducation.com

This site offers information on your child's development through the years, family activities, family news and topics, tips and resources, software downloads, message boards, ideas from parents, and advice from *familyeducation.com* experts.

www.lightspan.com

Lightspan offers plenty of information on education and parenting issues. The site is divided by grade level so you can track your child's progress through the years.

www.parentsoup.com

Parentsoup is not only parent-friendly, but also extremely informative. You can search topics arranged by your child's age group, and write to experts on a variety of topics.

Magazines

If your schedule or situation doesn't allow you to do your research on the web, you can have information delivered to your front door. Here are a few of the best parenting magazines we have found.

Family Life Magazine

The mission of this magazine—aimed at the parents of five to twelve year olds—is to help readers "embrace the unique challenges and joys of the busy years when your family is your life."

Offspring Magazine

Offspring, a recent addition to parenting magazines, shows its timeliness by including a heavy element of technology. There are reviews on software and websites, as well as articles on parenting. *Offspring* is published every other month.

Parents Magazine

Parents is one of the best-known monthlies for moms and dads. While this magazine focuses on the early years of your child's life, there are still plenty of relevant articles on older children and education issues.